CHANGING MEMORIES
INTO MEMOIRS

Changing Memories into Memoirs

A Guide to Writing
Your Life Story

Fanny-Maude Evans

BARNES & NOBLE BOOKS

A DIVISION OF HARPER & ROW, PUBLISHERS

New York, Cambridge, Philadelphia, San Francisco,
London, Mexico City, São Paulo, Sydney

To Paul

who taught me how to teach

CHANGING MEMORIES INTO MEMOIRS. Copyright © 1984 by Fanny-Maude Evans. All rights reserved. Printed in the United States of America. No part of this book may be used or reproduced in any manner whatsoever without written permission except in the case of brief quotations embodied in critical articles and reviews. For information address Harper & Row, Publishers, Inc., 10 East 53rd Street, New York, N.Y. 10022. Published simultaneously in Canada by Fitzhenry & Whiteside Limited, Toronto.

FIRST EDITION

Designer: C. Linda Dingler

Library of Congress Cataloging in Publication Data

Evans, Fanny-Maude.
  Changing memories into memoirs.

  Bibliography: p.
  Includes index.
  1. Autobiography. I. Title
CT25.E94 1984   808'.06692021   83–48787

ISBN 0-06-015293-1   84 85 86 87 88 10 9 8 7 6 5 4 3 2 1
ISBN 0-06-463599-6 (pbk.)   84 85 86 87 88 10 9 8 7 6 5 4 3 2 1

Contents

Acknowledgments

So many friends and colleagues have helped me in writing this book that it is impossible to list them all. I hope each will realize how grateful I am. Among them, I wish to thank especially:

Carol Amen, Shirley Climo, Kay Cruzic, Carole Davis, Anita Goldwasser, and Betty Goodman—present and former colleagues in my writers' workshop who listened patiently to each chapter, offering encouragement and criticism;

My students, for whom this book was written, for giving permission to use samples of their writing;

Patricia Chappell, program assistant in the Mountain View–Los Altos Adult School, for her advice;

Professor Lee Clark, in whose class the book was begun;

Jeanne Flagg, my editor, for her suggestions;

Those many writers and publishers who have allowed me to use excerpts from their work;

My husband, Paul, for surviving on frozen dinners, acting as my courier to photocopy centers and post offices, and for help with problem paragraphs.

Introduction

No matter who you are, where you were born, or where you live, you have a story to tell. Your life experiences happened to you and only you can record them. As you reach back in your memory you will discover adventures you had forgotten and highlights you would like to relive.

Do you remember the first time you drove a car? Did you grip the wheel with white-knuckled fingers? One writer forgot where the brake was when he approached a creek without a bridge. You can imagine how that adventure ended. Perhaps the first time you invited your in-laws to dinner is sharp in your mind. Or maybe your first day of school stands out in your memory, or your first job or your wedding day.

Every week I help my students bring memories like these alive. *Changing Memories into Memoirs* is an outgrowth of these classes. For, when I began teaching memoir writing, I found many books on how to write professionally but looked in vain for material on how people who haven't seriously thought about writing before should begin recording their experiences. My book is intended to fill this need. In its chapters I share the writing principles I have used in my own writing career. Some ideas may be new or different from those you learned in school, for the English language is rapidly changing. In this day of instant everything, your writing must be crisp and to the point if you want it to be read.

Saturday-night dances, groceries delivered to your door, and even the first space probe have almost disappeared from our memories. You can bring them alive when you share the sights and sounds, the scents and flavors of your past. Whether you write for friends and relatives, or your own satisfaction, or would like one day to reach a larger audience, I hope my book will inspire you to re-create the lights and shadows of your life.

1

Take a Look Backward

Everybody has memories but how do you change them into memoirs? And why?

First of all, perhaps you'd like to know just what memoirs are. If you look in your dictionary you'll find that memoirs can be an autobiography or a life story. They can also be a record of various happenings in your life. There lies the difference.

In writing your autobiography, you usually begin with the day you were born or shortly afterward and progress month by month, year by year, through your entire life. But your memoirs can begin anytime, anywhere. They can be as brief or as long as you like. For they are simply your memories, vignettes of highlight experiences you'd like to share. Whether you grew up early in the century or past the halfway mark doesn't matter. The day you are living now will be tomorrow's memory.

One student began her memoir writing while still in her twenties. She worked in a zoo nursery and kept a daily journal of the antics of bear cubs, baby monkeys, and infant tigers. Later she used the journal to write a delightful account of that period of her life.

Another student recorded his memories of a trip up the Amazon. He relived his encounters with exciting people and glimpses of exotic plants and rare animals as he wrote about them.

A woman who remembers washday as it used to be shared her story of her mother's first washing machine. They heated water on the kitchen stove, boiled the white clothes in a metal boiler, and shaved yellow soap into the wooden machine. With no electricity, "child power" pushed a wooden lever back and forth to move the wooden fingers that washed the clothes.

About now you're saying that's all just fine but you're not a writer.

You don't need to be. If you can write a letter you can write your memoirs. Just pretend you're chatting with a friend, telling a story as it happened. You can write it in any form you like. Diaries, journals, letters, sketches. Rose Kennedy, in *Times to Remember*, uses them all. She even adds verses and notes from her children and grandchildren.

Your stories can stretch across several periods in your life or paint one shining picture.

Maybe you were in love with your job. Perhaps it runs like a bright thread through your memories as it does for British writer James Herriot. All he wanted to do was to practice his skills as a veterinarian in the English countryside. His books take us along in his rattletrap car as he wrestles with belligerent bulls, pugnacious pigs, and coddled canines.

Or do vacations flash like film strips through your mind?

You don't have to ride your bike ocean to ocean or climb Yosemite's Half Dome to share exciting stories. In the 1920s my grandfather's British brother kept a journal when he traveled from London to New York and across the United States. The copy he sent my parents gave us many a laugh. He was amazed at pharmacies that served ice-cream sodas, fields watered from irrigation canals, and funeral parlors for the dead.

Yet a more recent vacation can be just as exciting.

A trip in a van, camper, or trailer, or a campout in the woods can be a real adventure. Some of you may remember the book and movie *The Long, Long Trailer*, by Clinton Twiss. The writer shares the fun, excitement, and even danger as a man and his wife learn to maneuver their trailer along narrow roads and around impossible mountain curves.

And what about holidays? Those special Christmas and Thanksgiving celebrations. Some were delightful, others near disasters. Like the time I had invited all the relatives for Thanksgiving dinner. When I took the turkey out of the oven the pan slipped from my hands and the bird slid on its glistening back clear across the kitchen floor. There's a Christmas, too, I'll never forget. I still laugh at the scene of my oldest aunt taking the broom to Cousin Jim when he had the nerve to light up a cigar in her living room. And, speaking of Christmas, surely you remember the shock you felt when that older brother or cousin told you who Santa really was.

The Glorious Fourth—what a memory that is! Did you pick dandelions for a penny a bucket or weed endless rows of onions to earn your fireworks as my brother and I did? Or, on July 3, did you set your alarm for midnight to be the first to throw out a giant firecracker?

What about the days when history exploded? They're indelibly etched on your mind. No history book can show how you really felt as you watched the moon landing. You were there, shivering with anticipation as the space module descended, the door opened, and the astronaut stepped out onto the face of the man in the moon.

You have much to write about wars, too. We've all lived through at least one. Vietnam with its Green Berets, napalm, campus riots, and draft-card burning. The shock of Pearl Harbor, Corregidor, ration coupons, blackouts. Perhaps you remember the first Armistice— the eleventh hour of the eleventh day of the eleventh month. Or Black Thursday when the stock market crashed. If you were there, you'll never forget the Great Depression with its patches on patches, bread lines, and hobos at your door.

By now, though, maybe you're saying all this writing sounds like a lot of work. Why should you bother? Nothing really very interesting ever happened in your life.

Don't you believe it. Your adventure in living is unique. Only you can tell it like it really was.

How did you survive that year you lost your job? How did you meet your spouse? What was your first date like? And what really happened on graduation night? All are a part of the history you've lived. But no one is going to hear about it unless you write it.

In ancient times tribal storytellers told and retold the tales of their ancestors' courage, determination, and stamina when faced with disaster. Later, grandparents lived with their sons and daughters or close by. With no TV or radio, they entertained children and grandchildren with stories of sod houses, buffalo hunts, prairie fires, square dances, and one-room schoolhouses.

Today, how many grandchildren even know their grandparents? Or their aunts and uncles? Relatives may live in another state, across the continent, or in a foreign country. And few modern parents have the time to tell their children the stories of their lives. Unless you belong to a family of squirrels, who stash away letters and diaries, the record of your life may be lost.

Anthropologist Margaret Mead said we have a duty to tell our stories, to leave a legacy for the young. People alive now have seen greater changes than ever before in history. Their children and grandchildren will see even more. How will they adjust to this whirlwind world?

The way we met and solved our problems can help them travel into the future with faith and courage. But they're not interested, you say. That's where you're wrong. Many of today's children and youth want to know about your life and the lives of those before you.

Recently a college freshman phoned her mother even though it was past midnight. She was so excited about her find in an old junk shop she couldn't wait till morning.

"What in the world is it?" her sleepy parent asked.

"Well, it's a smallish board and it has metal grooves on the front. The man I bought it from said you use it to rub out your washing. I just tried it on my undies. And it's absolutely the greatest."

Her mother exploded into laughter at the girl's description of an old washboard.

Other young people prize Franklin stoves, player pianos, oil lamps, battered milk cans, and butter churns. And they ask questions about the past. What was it like to ride in a rumble seat? How did it feel to be quarantined? How did you do your math without an electronic calculator? And what did you do in the evening before TV?

When my nephew disciplined his son by taking away his television privileges, the boy complained, "I bet your dad never made you give up TV."

His father smiled. "He sure didn't. We didn't have one when I was a kid."

Youngsters today can't imagine a world without it. Tell them about books you read, movies you saw, games you played. Remember how excited you were when Robinson Crusoe found footsteps on the beach? How you loved Shirley Temple in *The Little Colonel,* and what fun it was to play Rum Sheep Run on a warm summer night?

Share the worries and fears you had, too, in meeting the challenge of change. The first time you tried to use a dial phone, did it utterly confuse you? And did you worry when the gas furnace replaced the old coal burner, afraid it might blow up in the night? What about the first time you drove on a freeway? Did you grip the wheel and shudder, wondering if you were racing in the Indy 500?

Even learning to use new appliances can be overwhelming. When my neighbor remodeled her kitchen and laundry, she installed a new washer, dryer, dishwasher, and microwave oven. She studied the maze of buttons and dials and practiced pushing and turning each one. That night she woke screaming from a nightmare. She had dreamed she'd done everything in the wrong order and all the appliances had rushed out of their places to chase her around the house.

As you look back at your life your stories of meeting and adjusting to changes will not only inspire others. They may also provide a bonus for you.

In the introduction to his book *Dandelion Wine,* author Ray Bradbury says:

I took a long look at the green apple trees and the old house I was born in and the house next door where lived my grandparents, and all the lawns of the summers I grew up in, and I began to try words for all that. . . . Somehow I had to send myself back, with words as catalysts, to open the memories out and see what they had to offer.

You may find that your memories have a lot to offer. Reliving happy times brings back happy feelings. And you may discover, as I did, that memories not so happy lose their sting.

When I returned, after World War II, from living in Brazil, many of my memories of that country were far from pleasant. At that time Brazil was totally a man's domain and women had few rights. I began writing about my life, and as chapter by chapter my story unfolded, bitterness slowly changed to understanding. I could see, in examining my experiences, that my whole attitude had been wrong. I had been a guest in a foreign land. Even though I didn't like some of their ways, I had no right to judge the life of my hosts by mine.

As you take a look backward, be sure to mine the memories of parents and grandparents, too. Bring alive the friends, neighbors, and relatives who traveled through their years and yours.

I had a grandmother who said she'd either have a baby every year or cook but she wouldn't do both. She never cooked. Maybe your grandfather always planted his garden by the phases of the moon. Or a pioneer aunt fought marauding coyotes to save her chickens. Urge your older relatives to write down their stories, tell them to you, or put them on tape.

A friend spent nearly a year transcribing tape after tape her father recorded about his exciting years on an Idaho homestead. As she typed she became more and more intrigued with his life.

"Dad, why in the world didn't you tell us any of these stories before?" she wanted to know.

"Because you never asked," he replied.

Be sure you ask before it is too late. An old Chinese proverb says, "To forget one's ancestors is to be a brook without a source, a tree without a root."

Sometimes you don't have a chance to forget them. You never knew them. Like the girl in the portrait that hangs on my bedroom wall. Her young face, framed by curls piled high on her head, smiles serenely out from the gilded antique frame. Who was she? A great-great-great aunt? Or a cousin four or five times removed?

How I wish I knew! But by the time I inherited her picture those who could tell me were long gone. All I do know is that she is a link in my ancestral chain. Today more and more of us are searching for these links. Sparked by Alex Haley's dramatic story of his own search for roots, ancestor seekers spend hours poring over records in genealogical libraries. For ancestor hunting has now become the third most popular hobby in the United States.

But this hobby can be frustrating. One woman, looking at her pages of notes, said, "It's so disappointing. All these names and dates and nothing else. How I wish there were some way to put flesh on those old skeletons!"

You can't do much about ancestors who left no letters or diaries or journals. But you can see that those who come after you don't voice the same complaint. One day you will be an ancestor, a link in your own family chain. Will you be a strong link? Or a nameless face like the picture on my bedroom wall?

Begin now to think about the history you know and have lived. And take time to look at the memoirs of others. You'll find dozens of fascinating titles on the library shelves. Read them to see how the writers told their life stories. Some of the memoirs I've enjoyed are listed in the bibliography at the back of the book.

Keep a notebook, too, on your desk, your work table or beside your bed. Jot down bits and pieces of your past that pop into your mind. Later, as you read them over, you'll find many memories you can change into memoirs.

2

Trigger Your Memory

You've sharpened your pencils or uncovered your type-writer. You're ready to begin writing. But how do you choose which experiences to pull out of the attic of your memory?

Relax! Before you start, sit back and let your mind wander into the past. Close your eyes, if you like, and picture events as you recall them. Think of your life as a movie passing across a screen. Of course, like any movie, you can't see it all at once. Concentrate on one special period. Try to focus on a single scene. Rerun it again and again until it is so vivid you remember more than you see. Your senses come alive, and you can feel, hear, taste, touch, smell all that went with that long-ago experience.

Perhaps it will be your earliest memory. Was it the Christmas Santa brought a baby brother when you expected a puppy? What did you think when you first saw that squirming little bundle? Did you say, like one little girl, "Let's throw him in the garbage!" Or did you reach out and try to hold this precious new living doll?

And toys—do they loom large in your memory? A wagon, scooter, sled, or miniature iron steam engine? A tea set of tin or even of china or a doll with its very own cradle?

One of my friends still has her beautiful old doll. Now

it sits on her living-room sofa, but all the time she was growing up she never played with it. When she opened the box her aunt had sent on that long-ago birthday, her mother snatched up the doll.

"It's far too elegant for a young child," she said. She hung it high out of reach on the wall. There it stayed through the years as my friend gazed with longing eyes. She could never so much as touch it until at last her mother left the old house and the grownup daughter could take her doll down.

Games you played, what memories they bring. Ante Over, when you threw the ball as hard as you could across the roof to the other side. Red Light, Kick the Can, Pom Pom Pull Away, London Bridge Is Falling Down, Keep Away, and all kinds of tag. Remember when Truth or Consequences was a real game instead of a TV show? If you chose Truth, you had to answer questions like "Who is the first boy you kissed?" or "Which boy or girl do you want to marry?" If you chose Consequences they could be dire. You might have to leave rotten tomatoes on the principal's doorstep or find a garter snake to put in the teacher's desk.

Sometimes thinking of firsts may trigger other memories. What about your first day of school? Were you wide-eyed and excited, so eager to know all those new playmates you could hardly sit in your seat? Or did your mother leave you teary-eyed and sniffling as she went out the door?

One of my neighbors remembers her terror at even the thought of going to school. Older children had warned her about dunce caps, ruler slaps, and being expelled. She was sure the teacher must be a witch. When her mother left her in the classroom, she promptly ran home again.

The next day she fled to the attic and hid until it was much too late for school. Not until she finally made friends with another little girl did she decide that school wasn't so bad after all.

More firsts may flash by on your memory screen. Your first crystal set or radio, or the first time the movie *The Wizard of Oz* burst into color in the theater or on your television set. Your first date, dance, car, camping trip. The first time you stayed all by yourself or away from home overnight. And your first job. Can you ever forget that?

Mine didn't last very long. Our neighborhood grocer hired me when I was thirteen to help out in his store. It was a real problem to cut a pound and a half or any other amount from the big round cheese. It was all right if I cut too much, but poor me if I cut it under. That wasn't the reason I was fired, though. The good-natured grocer told me I could eat all the candy I wanted. He didn't know I was a chocoholic, and every time I passed the candy counter popped one into my mouth. Before long the store was out of chocolates and I was out of a job.

Mementos often bring back memories, too. Get out your box of souvenirs and keepsakes, treasures you've saved through the years. Take a new look at them. Why did you keep them?

Bundles of letters tied with ribbons. Yellowed news clippings, concert and theater programs. Lacy valentines you couldn't bear to part with. An orange May basket of braided crepe paper, flattened, now, in the box. What a memory it recalls! How far and how fast you had to run to catch the boy who hung it on your door! Remember the kiss you finally gave him? It was a real kiss even though he ducked and it landed on his forehead.

Dance programs. One of mine has a border of tiny blue flowers, a blue tassel and only one name filled in for every dance—the name of the man I later married.

An ivory fan, a carved bracelet, bone hairpins, an orchid pressed between sheets of waxed paper, a war medal or pocket watch. Even a faded ribbon can bring back a special memory. Writer Norma Wrathall shared a beautiful story about her own pink ribbon. When she tucked it in her hair, romance blossomed, for the ribbon attracted the tough little boy she'd secretly worshiped but who never before had given her a second look. When she wore the ribbon he chose her for the first time to play on his team.

In your growing-up years were you sometimes bitten by the collecting bug? You may remember a tiny sack of mini shells, for you specialized in only the smallest. Or rocks left over from the pile you once gathered. A bag of marbles in rainbow colors, butterflies you caught and mounted or a book of stamps from your very first collection. Even milk-bottle caps or strands of barbed wire mounted in a frame. Or maybe you preferred live specimens like lizards, snakes, toads, and grasshoppers. What became of them? One boy I know built little houses for each of his finds until his mother tossed them all out.

Photos, albums, and yearbooks—what a storehouse of memories they are! That picture of you in the pie-eating contest, blobs of custard smeared from ear to ear. The Christmas angel with the crooked halo you never could keep straight on your mop of hair. Pictures of a pompom girl, a football player, your graduation cap and gown all bring back the past.

And books. Perhaps your father, like mine, read to you. Today those books, their pages worn and dog-eared, are beloved treasures. *Swiss Family Robinson, Gulliver's*

Travels, Treasure Island, Robinson Crusoe spark delightful scenes of evenings around the old oak table, a bowl of
popcorn in the center, and Dad reading another chapter.
Maybe you acted them out as my brother and I did, and
not always happily. As Robinson Crusoe and his man Fri-
day, we tried to build a treehouse in the old maple in our
backyard. Crossing from one branch to another with a
board, my foot slipped and I crashed to the ground. All I
remembered was blackness and pain for days and days.
And, of course, that was the end of the treehouse.

Pain reminds us of medicine. What kind did you have
to take? Sassafras and raspberry-leaf tea? Boiled onion-
and-honey cough syrup? Blackstrap molasses in the
spring, mustard plasters and Musterole in the winter, aspi-
rin in strawberry jam, cod-liver oil in orange juice—all
were a part of home medicine.

No doubt at family reunions you still hear about all this.
And that's a marvelous place to gain more memoir material: stories your aunts and uncles and parents and grandparents tell, as well as sisters and brothers.

My favorite story is one about the day I was born. A
cousin of my mother's repeated it each time we met. He
was only fifteen when mother fought her way through
two-foot-deep snowdrifts to his house. She had expected
to find her midwife aunt there to deliver the baby. But,
in that day of few telephones, the aunt had gone on an
errand. As labor pains increased, my mother ordered her
young cousin to heat huge pots of water, for I wouldn't
wait. The embarrassed boy soon learned the real facts of
life when he had to assist at my birthing.

More tales pop up at class reunions. How you all laugh
when the master of mischief reminds you of the afternoon
he and all the other boys ran off at recess to rob a farmer's

melon patch. Or of the principal's old car you all helped to boost to the schoolhouse roof on Halloween night. And, as the master of mischief tells it, graduation wasn't all solemn. He remembers, when you tripped on your gown, the snicker that went through the line. Someone whispered the class motto, "We only stumble, we do not fall."

As these memories fly by, jot down brief notes. Later, look them over. Choose one you can see as vividly as a painting or photograph. Write everything you remember about it. Perhaps it's a story your grandmother told about living in a sod house. Don't worry if you don't know or have forgotten some of the details. Just write.

Later, read what you've written. No doubt you'll find you've begun an interesting memoir.

Maybe your description of a sod house is somewhat hazy. Don't be afraid to do a little research. Look in the historical section of your library. Ask the reference librarian to help. Or visit a local historical society and delve into its archives. You may want to write to one in the town where your grandmother lived or to the chamber of commerce. Often they'll send pages of information and perhaps even a picture of the very sod house you want to know about.

At the library, too, it's interesting to find out what was happening on the day you were born. Look up the newspaper microfilm for that date. Notice not only the news of the world and your town but also the ads. You'll be surprised to learn that a two-pound can of coffee was selling for 75¢ and a pound of hamburger for a dime.

You'll be surprised, too, when you see how one memory triggers another. As you write them down you'll soon find that you have more than a bagful to choose from in recording your adventures in living.

3

Twice-Told Tales—Tape Talking

You've finished your story about that ivory-and-silk fan your mother kept in its glass-topped box. But when you read it over it doesn't say what you mean. Here's where that modern tool the tape recorder can help you.

When you listen to your memoir on tape, it sounds a lot different from when you read it silently. All the rough spots seem to boom out and you hear your mistakes. Now you can sit down, rewrite, and improve your work.

A tape recorder may be the answer, too, if you are one of those people who can talk much more easily than write. One student tried for two years to put her memoirs down on paper. She had much to tell, for she had lived in San Francisco long before the Golden Gate Bridge was built. Yet, though she worked many hours with paper and pen, she could never write more than a few scattered notes.

In class she would begin to talk about what she wanted to write and go on and on with fascinating stories of dances in the redwoods, ferry rides across the bay, and picnics on an island. Finally, she bought a tape recorder. When she began to reminisce, her tape talks became a priceless record of her early life.

If, like this student, you tape your memoirs before you write, you'll save time in revising by doing a little planning before you begin. Jot down an outline of some sort.

List the four *w*'s—*who, what, when,* and *where*—and the main points in the story you want to tell. When you start to record, speak as if you were talking to someone.

You'll need to transcribe your tape, though, in order to revise it. If you love to talk, you'll probably find that you are far too wordy and must trim your sentences. And, of course, you'll need to add punctuation and put your work into paragraphs.

You may be tempted to leave the tapes as they are and let your children and grandchildren listen to them. Transcribing does take time but it's worth it. Even professional oral historians transcribe their tapes. For, no matter how careful you are, tapes can deteriorate or be accidentally erased. Far more people will enjoy your stories if they're written or typed. Your grandchildren will pick up a book or album from the coffee table and read or look through it when they wouldn't take time to get out a recorder to play a tape. And you can add photos, clippings, or other mementos to an album or scrapbook to make it more interesting.

Have your tape recorder ready, too, when you want to record someone else's memories. When Grandpa Roberts or Aunt Helen begins to talk about the day President Wilson was inaugurated or the blizzard that almost turned a fun sleigh ride into a tragedy, push the record buttons. For, unless you know shorthand, you won't be able to write fast enough to get their stories down.

When relatives get together at family dinners and on special occasions like reunions, holidays, and weddings, set up your tape recorder in an inconspicuous place. If the conversation seems to be too current, pass around old photos, clippings, albums. Play the "Do You Remember?" game.

One man heard a fascinating story when he showed a faded picture of a disheveled girl and a debonair young man leaning against a haystack.

"Aunt Hattie!" one of his great-aunts exclaimed. "That one! A real black sheep. Ran off to Australia with a sailor. Got tired of that hard life and came back to the States." She took a deep breath and went on with the story of a woman who scandalized the town. She wore men's overalls, cranked her own Model T, and built her own home at a time when a lady never did such things.

Sometimes you may want to arrange a special recording session with your father, grandmother, or a relative you haven't seen for a long time. Explain what you want to do and why. Again, it's a good idea to bring along family photos, clippings, or some family heirloom as a starter. And you may need to jog memories with a few questions:

Do you remember when the Baptist church burned down?

What about that winter when the snow came up to the windows?

I've heard about that Fourth of July parade when all the firecrackers went off at once. What happened?

Tell me how Uncle Vic won that medal in World War I.

Be careful to ask questions that require more than a yes or no answer or you may not get a story. And don't ask too many—just enough to get your aunt or uncle or grandparent talking. Be a good listener. If you want to hear more about something, make a note and ask about it later. Don't interrupt or you may turn the memory tap off.

Don't worry, either, when stories differ. We each remember according to our own reactions. And we tend to embroider our stories, to add or subtract to give flavor and feeling.

My cousin and I have long arguments about a chair my grandmother brought over from London as a bride. I distinctly remember what Grandmother said. She brought the chair on the ship because she wanted to be sure to have something to sit in when she went out to that godforsaken homestead in Texas. My cousin insists the chair was bought in New York. It's really not important. We each have our own memories. If our versions of the chair story differ, whoever reads them can put them together and choose the most likely.

If you are writing a formal family history, though, you must be as accurate as possible. Ask everyone who might remember. Read old journals, letters, and news clippings. Use the library and other research sources to find the right answers.

Perhaps you're now convinced you could make good use of a tape recorder but you don't have one. Which type should you choose?

Today they come in all shapes, sizes, and prices. Some mini- and micro-recorders are small enough to carry in your purse or pocket. They are usually more expensive than the larger models. To find out which one is for you, go to a reputable dealer and try them out.

Work all the controls. Switch from fast forward to rewind. Press the other buttons. They should be easy to see and to work. Put in a cassette and take it out. If one recorder seems confusing, try another. Buy the model that's simplest and easiest for you to operate, for you don't want to share one writer's unhappy experience. Using a new tape recorder, he pushed the rewind and fast-forward buttons instead of record and play. Of course he had nothing but a blank tape.

And don't worry about the quality of the sound. In

recording memories it's only important to understand the taped words clearly.

All tape recorders have controls for start, stop, record, rewind, and fast forward. Many have a tape counter, making it easier to find a particular place on the tape. An end-of-tape signal is convenient, too, to let you know when your tape has run out. And a battery-level indicator will show you when you need to change batteries. Of course, the more features a machine has the more it costs. Only you can decide which are necessary for your type of recording.

You don't need an expensive microphone. The built-in mike, though it does sometimes pick up noise from the motor, is fine for recording speech. Some models come with a small separate microphone you can use in a noisy place or for a distant speaker.

No matter which model you buy, you must take care of it. First of all, keep it clean. Dust is abrasive. After ten or twelve hours' use, you should clean the surfaces the tape passes over. You can buy an inexpensive special cassette to do this job, or you can do it yourself. Use a soft cloth or a Q-tip slightly moistened with alcohol. Remove the cassette, leaving the lid of the recorder open. Push the fast forward button down and wipe the heads. Next, press the play or on button. Wipe the rotating parts, brushing counterclockwise. Don't use a cassette until you're sure everything is completely dry.

About once a year or so, depending on how often you use it, take your recorder to a professional audio service shop for a checkup.

Your cassettes need some care, too. Put them back in their cases immediately after use to keep them dust free. Be sure to label them and keep an index if they are to be permanent. Store tapes away from heat and direct sun. Don't leave them in your car trunk, an attic, or a damp basement. And keep them away from loudspeakers, electric motors, or transformers—their magnetic fields can damage tapes. Even leaving tapes near a lamp cord for some time can cause deterioration.

Once you've bought your tape recorder and know how to take care of it, you still have to use it. Before you begin, you should be well acquainted with all its controls. Practice starting and stopping. Push record and play buttons, fast forward, and rewind. Insert and remove a cassette a few times so you won't put it in upside down or start on the wrong side. When you're ready to begin recording, check a few more details.

Be sure your cassette is working. Be sure, too, it's at the beginning, not at the end. And buy good cassettes—they don't jam. The type that is screwed together is better than the molded kind because you can take it apart if sometime you need to untangle it. Be sure to have an extension cord and extra cassettes, too. You never know when you may need them.

And carry a fresh supply of batteries. The stories you're recording may outlast your batteries. To find out how long you can use them, make a note when you put in new ones and when they run down. If they last one and a half or two hours you may be able to time changing batteries with changing cassettes. Remember, too, that recording uses them faster than playing.

Buy rechargeable nickel-cadmium batteries if possible. They cost more but die abruptly and do not wind down slowly, ruining your recording. The most exciting story may sound like chattering chipmunks if your batteries are dying. If you use regular batteries, choose the alkaline type and avoid those that are imported. They were fine when they were made, but they can lose energy in a ship's hold or in lengthy storage.

If you use a separate microphone, be sure it's plugged in and turned on. One student carefully checked his recorder. He put in a new cassette, and handed his father the mike. For an hour he listened in fascination to stories of coyotes, blizzards, and rattlesnakes on a South Dakota homestead. But, when he tried to play the cassette, all he could hear was the faint background noise from the motor. He had forgotten to flip the mike's on switch.

In using a microphone, place it on a book or something that won't vibrate. If possible, set it on a separate table so it won't pick up noise from the motor.

Be careful to stay away from fluorescent lights, fans, air conditioners, and all kinds of electric motors, too. Once I was interviewing a woman in her home. We sat at the kitchen table drinking coffee while I taped the story of her encounter with a rabid squirrel. Later, when I listened to the tape, I could barely hear her words. Though we hadn't noticed it, the noise of her refrigerator nearly drowned them out.

Perhaps you need to phone a brother or sister or cousin or aunt for information to complete the memoir you are writing. You're afraid, though, you won't be able to take notes fast enough.

Try telephone taping. You can buy a small suction cup that attaches to the earpiece of your phone. It does have one drawback—it may pick up a hum. If this is so strong it interferes with the recording, there are several remedies.

Check to see if your phone is near an electrical cord. Move the phone around and find a spot where there is less hum. Using batteries in your recorder helps to reduce the hum, too. If you're using a cord, you can try turning the plug over.

Of course, before you place your call, you'll need to check to see if everything's working. Dial Time or Weather, tape the answer, and listen to your tape. Be sure to erase it, though, before you dial your number.

Once I played a telephone interview for a group of friends. To my embarrassment, when I turned on the recorder, it began, "The time is two thirty-three and forty seconds. The time is two thirty-three and forty-one seconds."

Mindful of Watergate, you may have some questions about telephone taping. Is it legal? Don't you have to use a beeper?

It all depends on where you live. Federal law requires you to tell a person he or she is being taped. That's all. Many phone companies insist you need a beeper. However, this varies from state to state. Check the front of your telephone directory. Unless it definitely states that taping without a beeper is *illegal,* go ahead as long as you tell the person being taped.

Now let's practice. Set up your tape recorder, or borrow one. Record that story you wrote. As you listen to it, check your paper. Make notes where you need to rewrite. Then revise.

For more practice, schedule a tape talk with your sister, cousin, or brother. Record a story as he or she tells it, remembering to ask a few starter questions. Transcribe the tape, adding or subtracting details as needed, and you'll have material for another memoir.

4

The Plan's the Thing

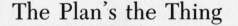

You've taped your memoir and played it back. Somehow, though, it sounds more like a band that keeps changing its beat than the story you wanted to write. What now?

You need a plan. Writing is like going on a journey. If you don't know where you're going you'll never get to your destination. You may even get stuck in a detour. Your plan is a map pointing the way, but it's a map you'll have to make for yourself.

Maybe, though, you're the sort of person who wants to just sit down and write. After several lessons, one student complained, "I can't seem to write any more. I keep thinking about the principles of writing you've taught, and they get in the way."

Don't be like this student. Write in whatever way is easiest for *you*. If you like to sit down and pour it all out on paper, do that. But, when you've finished, go back and organize. You may find words you don't need, sentences out of order, and paragraphs in wrong places. If you just can't seem to form a plan at all, write a letter, telling your story to a friend. Either way, you'll need to organize when you've finished.

Writer Isaac Bashevis Singer feels that he needs a plan. He says:

If I were to sit down with no plan at all, I would feel that the reader would know after ten or twelve pages. Once you begin to write, some of your plans are torn to pieces anyhow, but you have to be consistent. You cannot give a man a red beard and change it to a black one ten pages later. There is a Yiddish story about this: a man meets another man in the Lower East Side in New York. He tells him, "What happened to you, Rappaport? You used to be a tall man; now you are a small man. You used to have a black beard; now you have a red beard. Is this what this country has done to you?"

The second man replied, "My name is not Rappaport."

"So, you have changed your name, too?"

Most of you, like Isaac Singer, will need to know where you're going before you begin. Your plan can be simple sentences and phrases jotted down on a piece of paper, ideas filed in your head, or a real outline. Don't panic at that word. Forget your fifth-grade teacher, Miss Blanche Wilson. She's not looking over your shoulder now. Forget the Roman numerals I, II, III, with their A, B, C subheads. Let your outline be as informal as you like. It's for you alone. And don't follow it too closely. You are not tied to the outline. If your writing begins to change direction, keep writing. If it strays too far, you can always make corrections afterward.

Every plan has a beginning, a middle, and an end. And, no matter what kind of plan you choose, you need to know where you are going and what you want to say. You need a guideline sentence to tell us the main idea or theme of your memoir.

In "Rice in Our Teacups," my story about a stay in a Japanese inn some years ago, the guideline is:

Long before Japanese inns, called ryokans, catered to west-erners, my husband and I wanted to find out about the world hidden behind the shoji screens.

And in "Chicken Soup" a student tells us where she is going with this sentence:

During my childhood, my digestive system periodically sloshed with chicken soup.

Another student, in a story about the old ways farmers had to forecast weather, uses this guideline:

With no radios, barometers, TV or weather forecasting, we learned much about weather patterns.

Each of these sentences tells us what the story is about. It's easy, though, to forget your guideline and wander off in another direction. To help you remember, type or print it and tape it above your desk. It will constantly remind you to stay on the track.

Now that you have your guideline, what kind of plan are you going to follow?

In memoir writing you'll probably choose the chronological plan more often than any other. It tells your story just as it happened. As in fiction, you begin with some sort of problem. It doesn't have to be a death-defying adventure. It can be as simple as surviving your first day on a job or as dramatic as running from a wall of water in a flash flood. You use scenes, characters, dialogue, and suspense, and build to a climax.

"Rice in Our Teacups" follows this chronological plan.

GUIDELINE: Long before Japanese inns, called ryokans, catered to westerners, my husband and I wanted to find out about the world hidden behind the shoji screens.

PROBLEM: Our travel agent tried to discourage us. "Those Japanese inns don't care much about western tourists," he said. In Tokyo, we asked the Japan

Travel Bureau to book us into the Jingu Bashi
Ryokan.

SETTING: Looks more like a barn than a hotel, I thought.
I stepped across puddles on the wet rock floor,
freshly washed, I'd read, in honor of new arriv-
als. At the back of a long hall, on a wooden step,
I could see rows of slippers in rainbow colors.

CHARACTERS: Above them, on a wide wooden platform, a
man in shirtsleeves and a youngish woman in a
gray kimono bowed and smiled. Two little
maids right out of Gilbert and Sullivan giggled
beside them.

DIALOGUE: Paul leaned over to pick up our bags. The maids
twittered like robins who'd lost their worms.
They pulled at the handles. Paul held on.

"You'd better give up," I said. "They look like
they're ready to cry."

"These bags are too heavy for them," he protested.

The story continues with anecdotes relating our mistakes as we tried to adjust to Japanese customs. Stepping
on the tatami mat without removing slippers, pouring tea
into our rice bowls, refusing to let the little maid undress
us were only a few of our errors. Each time we did the
wrong thing the suspense mounted, until, finally, we
made the worst mistake of all.

CLIMAX: Like a mind-bending drug the boiling bath
habit seemed to grow. And we finally decided
we couldn't wait each day for Sumako, our little
maid. We'd go it alone.

Paul tapped outside the dressing room. All
was quiet. We peeked in. The sliding screen to
the bath beyond was closed as usual. Every-

thing seemed clear. We took off our kimonos. I was folding them when the screen slid back. A Japanese grandmother dressed only in her long gray hair bowed politely. She motioned to Paul to come in. His face turned as red as a July sunburn. He grabbed his kimono and backed toward the door so fast he forgot to open it.

We decided there must be an order for the bath. Next time we'd wait for Sumako.

PROBLEM SOLVED: We stayed a week at the Jingu Bashi and gradually learned what we should and should not do. Caught up in the frantic rush of the world's largest city, we looked forward each evening to the inn's serenity and solitude. And to Sumako's attentive pampering.

ENDING: In spite of our travel agent's warning we were glad we'd stayed in a ryokan. Behind the shoji screens we had tasted the flavor of Japan and found it a delight. And we had already booked into another ryokan at the next stop on our itinerary.

> "Rice in Our Teacups" by Fanny-Maude Evans, *PEN*, February, 1972

This is an easy way to write your memoir. But what if it isn't chronological? You want to include experiences that didn't happen exactly in order.

Try a plan often called the *train of thought*. It resembles a railroad train with a cowcatcher in front, a locomotive, cars, and a caboose. The cowcatcher grabs our attention, often with the guideline. The locomotive pulls us into the story. Each car follows the lead of the locomotive and takes us farther on our journey. As we proceed, anecdotes, experiences, or facts build interest, with the most exciting or dramatic at the last. The caboose, of course, is the ending, sometimes mentioning the guideline again, adding a new fact, or referring to the beginning.

Student Jayne Vosti used the *train of thought* method when she wrote "Chicken Soup."

COWCATCHER: During my childhood, my digestive system periodically sloshed with chicken soup. It was absolutely a cure-all for everything from a sniffle to pneumonia.

LOCOMOTIVE: I had more than my share of childhood diseases because, according to my relatives, I was very fair. Consequently, I was overly protected with no boisterous playing, no getting in drafts, never going barefoot. Raised like a hothouse flower, I became one.

FRONT CAR: Until I went to high school, the green bed-
(SETTING)   room was my hospital room. The wallpaper fortunately had an irregular pebble-like pattern. Mosaic would describe it. My greatest pastime was seeing different faces in it, always horrid, ugly old men. . . . Some had noses like an ear of crooked corn, or ears like a pock-marked donkey, their eyes either crossed or one looking up and the other down.

SECOND CAR: No sooner was I settled in bed than in would come the cup of nauseating chicken soup. No use arguing. I would drink it. Cup after cup every two hours. Of course I'd get better—nature took care of that.

THIRD CAR: I'd get almost paranoid about chickens. I could hear them cackling outside my bedroom and I kept wondering which one was in the pot. I absolutely refused to eat any of the meat. To

	this day I can't eat chicken in any form. People chewing on a leg or wing send goose bumps up my spine.
FOURTH CAR: (CLIMAX)	The thing that really finished me with chickens was my aunt deciding it was time I learned how to kill the little creatures. She handed me a chicken by the neck and a large knife. I started cutting but I couldn't finish and the chicken ran away bleeding.
CABOOSE: (REFERS TO BEGINNING)	After that everybody was sure I was a weak, delicate child. Whenever I looked a little pale, it was back into the green room and more chicken soup.

Perhaps, though, you want to write a piece that won't fit into either of these plans. You want to remember all the games you played and how you played them; the medicines you had to take and how they tasted; the different holidays and how you celebrated. What kind of plan can you use?

The easiest of all—a list. This simply has a beginning with a guideline sentence and perhaps a paragraph or two of explanation. Then you go on to list the various games you played, explaining what they were. Or the medicines your mother made you take, when and what for. And holidays you remember—what you did, with whom, and where. Finally, in the ending you can state your guideline again, or circle back to the beginning, or come to some conclusion about your experiences.

Student Zella Edwards used the list plan when she wrote "Sky Farmers," a story about old-time methods of weather forecasting.

| BEGINNING: | We were called Sky Farmers when I married and moved to the ranch in 1921. A Sky Farmer |

had to depend on whatever the good Lord sent us from the sky. Having no irrigation and only a small gasoline engine to pump water when the windmill failed to turn, we had to be very careful. No one will ever know how many prayers we prayed, especially when we had three dry years, 1923, 1924 and 1925.

GUIDELINE: With no radios, TV barometers or weather forecasting, we learned much about weather patterns.

EXPLANATION: Some came from Indians, some from the Almanac, some from personal observations. Some even came from the Bible, like Matthew 16:2, 3: "When it is evening, you say, it will be fair weather for the sky is red. And in the morning, it will be foul weather today; for the sky is red and lowering."

She continues by listing twenty-six more weather-forecasting signs from the sky and ends this way:

ENDING: These are the common signs of weather I remember as a Sky Farmer. "Ours not to reason why, Ours but to do or die"—and we almost did.

When you've decided on your plan and written your memoir, you may want to use a checklist to see if you have arrived at your destination. Ask yourself these questions:

Do I have a plan?
Did I follow it?
What is my guideline?
Does something happen between the beginning and the end of my story?
Did I say what I wanted to say?

To practice recognizing different plans, check magazine articles you read. See if you can fit them into one of the plans. Sometimes they may be a combination of two, or have only a simple beginning, middle, and end. Try to find the guideline to see where the story is going. Decide whether or not it arrives.

Then choose a plan and write your own memoir. See if you can set out on a writing journey and stay on the road until you reach your destination.

5

Baiting the Hook—Beginnings

You lean back in your chair as memories flit like movie scenes across your screen of life. Some are of long ago. They seem faded and out of focus. Others are as vivid as the most recent space shot. Suddenly you see a picture so bright and exciting that it stops the reel. It's so clear that you think it will be an easy piece to write.

Yet you sit and stare at the wall. In spite of the clear picture you can't seem to begin.

You're not alone. Professional writers often crumple page after page as they struggle with that first sentence. They may write dozens of beginnings, for they know the beginning is the most important part of their writing. It must have a snap-to-attention quality to attract a reader rushing by.

It's like news you've just heard and can't wait to share. You see a friend jogging past your house. You run out but she waves and calls, "See you later. Can't stop now."

"Wait!" you yell. "The president's been shot!"

She skids to a stop. Her hurry vanishes.

Just so your beginning or lead, as professionals call it, must make us skid to a stop. Writers often compare the first sentence to a baited fishhook. It must lure us and hook us quickly to hold our attention. It should create suspense, make us wonder what's coming. And it should be something familiar, if possible. Like this lead:

It was after midnight as our car fishtailed across the ice-slick road into a deep snowbank.

All of us have had the experience of a car slipping and skidding on a road. We'll read on to find out what happened.

Now, perhaps, your first sentence pops into your mind. You write it down. Your lead begins to take shape. Yet you wonder how long it should be. The shorter the better. After all, its purpose is to attract our attention. Sometimes your beginning needs to be only one or two sentences.

"I saw the Easter rabbit, I really did," begins a story about a little girl's search, year after year, to find the Easter bunny. This simple lead intrigues us. We want to know how, when, and where the child saw that Easter rabbit.

Generally, though, a beginning is at least one paragraph.

Sometimes my pioneer grandmother felt like she was in jail. And that was when she would do something so shocking, in that day, that the neighbors would talk about it for weeks. She would leave the baby with my grandfather, take the buggy and drive off to the city alone for a weekend of fun.

What did she do there? What happened when she came home? You'd like to find out, wouldn't you?

Once in a while you may need a beginning with more than one, two, or three paragraphs. But be careful. You have to keep building suspense to hold our interest. I used a long lead in my story about an experience in Nepal.

Of all places to get sick, I thought, Nepal has got to be the worst. I staggered out of bed, my breath puffing out like steam in the chilly hotel room. Pain stabbed between my ribs, and I clutched my husband's arm to keep from falling.

"Got to get you to a hospital," he said. I shivered with more than cold.

"That's the last thing I want, Paul. Why I've heard they still use witchcraft to treat a stomach-ache here. Can't you find me a real doctor? One that speaks English?"

He hunched down on the bed. "I've tried," he said. His voice sounded tired. "I even went to the consul. But his doctor doesn't treat tourists. And the only other American I've heard of is out at that mission hospital."

"Well, I'm not going to any old mission hospital," I snapped. "It's probably as primitive as the rest. Anyway, I know I'll feel better pretty soon."

But I didn't. Hour after hour the pain grew. When I could no longer tolerate even a small sip of water, Paul bundled me into the back seat of a wheezing taxi.

Fear blended with pain as we bumped along a rutted road toward the mission hospital.

Frightening thoughts leaped into my mind. What was I getting into? What kind of hospital?

"A Blanket of Love," *Lutheran Women,* April, 1978

You won't often need a beginning as long as that one. But, no matter how long your lead is, remember to include the four *w's—who, what, when,* and *where.* The most important are *who* and *what.* A student writer packed all four into this beginning.

August 18, 1933, is a date I will never forget for it changed my life.

On that Saturday evening, I and my friends, the three Mooney girls, decided to go dancing at the Larkspur Bowl near Sausalito. Also called the Rose Bowl, it was a fun place to go.

"The Winker" by Helen Drechsler, *Silhouettes of the Past*

We find out *when*—August 18, 1933—in the first sentence. Next, we learn *who*—the writer and the three Mooney girls. Then *what*—dancing—and *where*—the Larkspur Bowl near Sausalito.

Perhaps you may feel you have a first sentence or paragraph that hooks us so hard we can't wriggle away. But you need something more. Remember your guideline sentence we studied in the last chapter? It's an important part of your beginning, for it tells us what your story is about.

"I saw the Easter rabbit, I really did" lets us know that in the story the writer is going to tell us how, when, and where she saw that Easter bunny.

In the piece about my pioneer grandmother, the guideline is:

She would leave the baby with my grandfather, take the buggy and drive off to the city alone for a weekend of fun.

We know right away we're going to read about Grandma's unorthodox behavior.

And in the Nepal story we don't know for sure what direction we are going to travel until almost the end of the lead.

"What was I getting into? What kind of hospital?"

You know, now, that the beginning of your memoir should be as short as possible and contain the four *w*'s, or at least *who* and *what*, and your guideline. But you still can't seem to get started.

Try an anecdote. Everyone loves a story. To begin a piece about heroes in his family, one man wrote an incident about an aunt.

Any time our family gets together, we talk about heroes. We don't call them that because they're not famous, but they're heroes just the same. Like Aunt Zonie. She had more spunk than any of us. We often visited her homestead on a fork of the Gunnison River. One morning, we were coming up from fishing. All of a sudden she shoved me out of the path. She grabbed a stick and jabbed it down on the head of a big old rattler. Then she pulled up her petticoats and stomped it to death.

Don't you want to hear more about Aunt Zonie?

We all like a surprise or even a shock to arouse our interest, too. The next beginning promises both.

Trev's ESP must have been working overtime that July morning. Or maybe it was the ugly look of the sea that warned the youngest member of the crew to prepare for trouble.

Great gray breakers dashed their foam against the grotesque pinnacles rearing above Virgin's Bay. Like giant tikis they cast grim shadows over the island of Fatu Hiva.

"We'll never make it," Trev said.

The captain turned. "Got to," he barked. "Coral poison is spreading up the boy's whole leg. Got to get him to a hospital. He looks like he's dying."

Did they get the boy to the hospital? Did he die? You won't put this story down until you find out.

Maybe the setting of your memoir is so unusual it will attract attention. Like this one:

Sand. Sand. Sand. As far as I could see, for miles and miles, there was nothing else. I had read about this Colorado dust bowl but its desolation was beyond my wildest imaginings. From the door of my shack I could not see a tree nor a plant nor a rock anywhere. Only the endless drifts of sand creeping like some prehistoric monster into the roads, over the fences and up to the windows. I shivered in spite of the shimmering heat. How could I survive the next three years in this place? Would the menacing sand bury me, too?

I wonder, don't you? How did the writer survive?

Quite often you'll be tempted to start with a statement. That's fine but you may find it's hard to grab our attention with this kind of lead. It can be done but the statement must be striking and unusual. As this one is:

Just before my fortieth birthday four words changed my whole life.

What were those words? You'd like to know, wouldn't you?

Sometimes you can use dialogue to arouse interest. We all like to hear people talking whether we know them or not. Many of us are born eavesdroppers. In a story about wearing middy blouses, writer Robin Worthington began with a conversation.

The other day two of my teenage daughters were discussing their school wardrobes. "I'm going to buy an Indian import bedspread and make a dress out of it," said the senior.

"I'm going to make a long Levi's skirt with a patchwork inset," said the freshman.

"Bedspreads? Levi's? What ever happened to the good old middy?" I asked.

"Midi? You mean a midi skirt?"

"No, I mean a middy blouse—you know, with a sailor collar. Every public high school girl in Seattle used to own one."

> "Whatever Happened to the Good Old Middy Blouse?," Seattle *Post-Intelligencer* *Northwest*, September 15, 1974

This conversation recalls, for many of us, those days when we or our schoolmates wore middy blouses, and we'll read on to share the writer's experience.

Another type of lead you might want to try is the question. Ask it and let your story answer it, as student Charles Reed did in his memoir, "A Lesson in Silver."

Did you ever buy an ingot of silver? Neither did I until my boss in Detroit sent me 137 one-dollar silver certificates to be redeemed at the San Francisco mint in silver ingots.

Why did he want silver bars? Where did he acquire the dollar bills with the printed words "Redeemable in Silver"?

Silhouettes of the Past

We're all interested in silver and money and we'll turn the page to learn the answers to these questions.

Maybe, though, you'd like to use a quotation to begin your memoir. Once in a while you may find one that is exactly right. Use it, but be sure it's unusual enough to whet our interest. A story about graduation began with just such a quotation.

> Two by two, side by side;
> On they come like automation.
> Two by two, side by side;
> Noah's Ark? No. Graduation!

Excerpt from "Pas de Deux" by Robert Orben, *Reader's Digest*, June, 1981 (Item originally appeared in *Orben's Current Comedy*, May 23, 1974.)

And what about statistics? Should you ever use them in your beginning? Most people consider statistics so boring that they tend to skip over numbers. But sometimes, especially if you're writing about a great disaster you remember, like the San Francisco earthquake or the Galveston flood, or something an astonishing number of people have or do, you need statistics. As I did in my piece about my color-blind husband.

Do you like rainbows? If you don't you're probably color-blind. There are more than 8,000,000 people in the United States who can't see all the rainbow colors. Most of them are men and I'm married to one of them. When I met Paul back in Depression days, I had no idea he couldn't tell a ripe strawberry from a green one.

> "A Different Kind of Rainbow" by Fanny-Maude Evans,
> *Elks Magazine,* November, 1972

Try using all of these leads. If one doesn't seem to suit your story, try another. Spend time on that first sentence and paragraph, for they are the most important. Write a dozen or more beginnings if you need to. Practice writing them in your head while you're driving down the freeway, waiting in the dentist's office, or walking to the store.

Now, go back to the scene that stopped your memory reel. Write a beginning so vivid it will make your son or daughter or grandchild slide to a stop, pick up your memoir, and read it.

6
Wrapping It Up—Endings That Satisfy

※

The memory scene that flashed across your mind was so vivid that you've been able to finish the whole story. But, as you read it over, something seems to happen. Like the camel crossing the desert, it gets drier and drier as it goes on and on.

What's wrong?

You probably didn't know where to end. And that's not surprising. Good endings are often hard to find. Yet your last sentence is almost as important as your first. Endings go with beginnings. And, like beginnings, you can learn to write good ones.

What is a good ending? Even editors are vague about answering this question. They do agree, though, that your final words must do one thing—satisfy the reader. How many times have you read a story and felt cheated at the end? Somehow you were left with an unfinished feeling.

Like one man who knew exactly the way he wanted a piece to conclude. "I like a story that ends finally," he said to his daughter.

"What do you mean?" she asked.

"I want the writer to either marry 'em off or murder 'em."

A good ending should stop before we expect it to. It's like a movie you're watching. Maybe it's a western and the hero and heroine finally escape from the bad guys. Abruptly "The End" flashes across the screen. It takes you by surprise. The lights go on and you sit there staring for a moment. Then you smile as you realize that the future of the hero and heroine is left up to you.

You know when you like an ending. But how do you write one that will satisfy your reader?

Sometimes you may want to use a new idea or new information to complete your memoir as I did in the account of my experience in a Nepali hospital.

As pain decreased and strength returned, my bed no longer seemed hard. And I didn't feel the cold draft in my room. I was too busy looking for special needs my church at home might be able to fill.

I even hated to think of leaving. For the blanket of love spread over my bed had warmed not only my body. It had warmed my soul as well.

> "A Blanket of Love" by Fanny-Maude Evans,
> *Lutheran Women*, April, 1978

When you're looking for a good ending, think of beginnings. You can use the same types. Perhaps an anecdote will really wrap up your story. Like this one about an elderly artist with a zest for living.

Harry Lieberman, 101 years old, recently went to a doctor for a checkup. The doctor announced, "Harry, you can go out and buy yourself a new suit."

"Doc," Harry said, "on my way to see you I already stopped in and bought a suit. The salesman says it will last me a good ten years."

> Excerpt from "Age: 101—Motto: 'Go Do!' " by Peggy Mann,
> *Reader's Digest*, August, 1978

Do you like surprises? They're good in endings, too. You can use a surprise or shock to make a final point or emphasize some truth in the memoir you are writing. A story of a busload of school children stranded in a fierce blizzard ends this way:

When rescuers pushed open the frozen bus doors, they were amazed to find that all the children had survived. They were hungry and cold but none had suffered more than a few frostbitten toes. Sixteen-year-old Diane had kept them jumping and clapping and playing action games all night. But where was the bus driver who had faced the blizzard to go for help?

Searchers found his body buried in drifts just ten feet behind the bus.

Once in a while you can use your setting to complete your story, especially if it relates directly to your writing. I chose this type of ending in a memoir about living in Brazil during World War II.

Our plane rose smoothly into the air. I looked down at the huge city spreading out in an ever widening pattern of new homes and expanding industries. I remembered its comparison to an adolescent boy. The great metropolis was still growing and still plagued with shortages. Yet, as I thought of the tremendous progress of the past three years, I realized that São Paulo was nearing the end of its adolescence.

As the outline of the city faded into the drifting clouds, I hoped that we, too, had grown. Perhaps we had learned, at last, to measure the people and their culture by their own meter and not by our yardstick imported from the States.

Maybe, though, you're thinking a simple statement would be the easiest way to wrap up your story.

It does look easy. Yet it can be the hardest of all to write. A statement can be as dull as a doctoral dissertation if you're not careful. It should have only one thought and it should be brief. You must revise and revise and cut and cut to make a statement ending interesting. I learned this lesson in writing and rewriting the end of my short account of a surprise dinner. I had considered my neighbors unfriendly and almost hostile until they brought over a feast from their own kitchens to feed my unexpected guests. My first ending went like this:

As the neighbors turned away, tears wet my face. Happy tears, this time. Happy and grateful for these kind and understanding women.

Somehow, that didn't seem right. I struggled with several more and finally decided I had what I wanted.

Tears again wet my cheeks. Happy tears. For I knew, now, that God had not deserted me. When I most needed it, he had sent these kind and understanding women to bring me this gift of neighborly love.

But the *Guideposts* editor didn't like it. He revised it.

Tears wet my cheeks, happy tears. For I saw then, how often God works through people to carry out kind and loving acts. Suddenly, I was no longer a stranger.

"A Very Special Dinner," *Guideposts*, August, 1975

I agreed with his revision. That final statement says it all.

Another way to complete your memoir is by writing dialogue. Everybody likes to hear people talking. I used conversation to end one short *Catholic Digest* piece. Reluctantly I had enrolled my small daughter, Dixie, in a new school on Valentine's Day. All afternoon I had worried that she would feel left out when the valentine box was opened. But she came skipping into the house with three valentines.

When she wasn't looking I held them up to the light. Faint lines dented the shiny surfaces as if something had been erased. I had to squint to make out, "To my teacher." "To Mrs. Elmer." And a few letters, "For m– t–ac—r."

Dixie danced toward me. She grabbed the valentines and hugged them to her. "I have three friends," she bubbled. "And a nice teacher."

"Yes you do," I said, smiling.

"A Valentine for Dixie," *Catholic Digest*, February, 1976

Sometimes, too, a question makes a good ending. Especially if you want to leave your reader with a new thought. The story about my husband's color blindness ends this way.

Though color blindness isn't a big handicap, I'm sure Paul would enjoy seeing all the colors. And he wouldn't buy green tissue for our pink bathroom. Nor call a green Volkswagen "that orange bug." But he might be disappointed about a few things. Like my eyes. He calls them brown though I've told him they're not. What would he say when he found out I'm right? And they are not brown at all but really green?

"A Different Kind of Rainbow,"
Elks Magazine, November, 1972

You may be asking your own question, now. Can you use a quotation in an ending?

Only if you can find one that gives exactly the right punch. Student Rozilla Reed used an appropriate quotation to end her memoir about the hectic adventures of two naïve young women visiting New York.

As the old saying goes, "The Lord takes care of fools and children." You may have your choice of the category we belonged in.

"Innocents Abroad in New York," Silhouettes of the Past

Once in a while you might need to use a statistic to finish your story. But, just as in beginnings, it must be so startling or unusual that your reader will feel it's absolutely necessary. Writer Jim Bishop, in "The Happy Hacker," his tongue-in-cheek piece about the miseries of golf, ends this way.

At present there are about 15 million hackers in this nation. There are almost that many wives who think their husbands are out there having fun. But any duffer who comes home convinced that he enjoyed himself has either just played his first round, or his last.

Excerpt from "The Happy Hacker" by Jim Bishop,
Reader's Digest, August, 1978
(Article originally appeared in Tropic Magazine, April 2, 1978)

One of the best ways of all to end your writing is to use an echo. There are two types. One repeats your guideline or a thought from the beginning. The last paragraph of the memoir about the Japanese ryokans refers to the travel agent's warning and to the shoji screens mentioned in the beginning.

In spite of our travel agent's warning, we were glad we'd stayed in a ryokan. We'd experienced that atmosphere of strangeness and charm and devoted personal attention we'd read about. Behind the shoji screens we had tasted the flavor of Japan and found it a delight. And we had already booked into another ryokan at the next stop on our itinerary.

"Rice in Our Teacups," PEN, February, 1972

Another type of echo ending repeats a word or phrase used several times in your story. I did this by repeating the word magic in "The Magic Map."

A map can be a traveler's best friend, indispensable for locating roads, rivers and restaurants. But it can be more: it can have a touch of *magic*.

You find the word again in other paragraphs.

Even in bustling Tokyo the *magic* continued. On a frosty winter afternoon we shivered on a corner while we studied our city map till our eyes ached.
In Germany the map worked its greatest *magic* of all.

Finally, the ending echoes the word *magic* again.

And so it went. In every country the *magic* led us to our destinations. But it did more. It overcame the language barrier and introduced us to the people, as well as the places, of other nations.

Fanny-Maude Evans, *Odyssey*, March/April, 1981

These endings are all very well if you're writing a short memoir. But what if you're working on a book-length account of a great experience or adventure in your life? How do you conclude each chapter?

Use a cliff hanger, an ending that leaves us dangling in suspense. You ask a question or create a mystery that makes us want to keep on reading.

In the story about my life in Brazil, I ended Chapter 4 like this:

The bell buzzed. I looked out just in time to see a package wrapped in newspaper come sailing over the hedge. A boy on a bicycle pedaled furiously past the gate as I ran to pick up the mysterious bundle.

Remember, no matter what type of finish line you choose, you must be sure it leaves us satisfied. For practice in recognizing good endings, look at those in magazines. See how other writers wind up their writing. What types do they use? Do they leave you with a satisfied feeling? Or do you wish they had ended sooner, or later?

Go back to that story that seemed to drag. Look at your last page. Find a spot near the end that gives you a feeling of surprise or joy, or a new idea. Cut everything else off.

S-T-O-P! Remember the camel. Don't go on and on as you become drier and drier.

7

A Title Is a Teaser

You've found an ending that seems to satisfy but the space above the first sentence is blank. You couldn't think of a title. Besides, do you really need one?

Yes, you do. Your title is the first thing your readers see. It lures them to take the bait offered in your beginning and often determines whether they read your memoir or pass it over.

What do you do before you buy a magazine at your market or news stand?

You turn to the table of contents and look through the titles, don't you? Are you interested in cooking? Then, no doubt, you'd buy the magazine with such titles as "Summer Fruit: Kiwi to Quince," "Symphonies from the Kitchen," or "Overnight Breads for Busy Bakers." Maybe car, radio, or scientific topics are more to your liking. Such titles as "Hotter Engines, Softer Rides," "Great Stereo Sounds," or "The Atomic Man" would interest you. Or perhaps you just want to read a good adventure story like "Buried Alive," "Runaway," or "She Fell Among Thieves."

See how your title is like a billboard? It must attract attention and arouse curiosity. Wouldn't you be tempted to read "The Poison That Fell from the Sky," "Irreverent Recollections of a President's Daughter," or "The Phony Felons of Fleetsie"?

Novelist Helen Arvonen, in an article in *Writer's Digest*, tells of her experience with one title. Flipping through a magazine one afternoon, she stopped as she read "Barking Made Easy." Intrigued, she decided to save that piece for dessert after she'd finished the other articles. Finally, turning again to the page, she blinked at "Banking Made Easy." Tossing the magazine aside, she said, "Who cares about banking?"

Be sure your reader will care about your title. Don't let it be just a label. "A Winter Morning," "The Inn," "The Babysitter," "Dan's Journey" are labels. You don't want to read about just any winter morning, an inn, babysitter or even a boy named Dan, do you?

But you can change these labels into titles that tell us what your subject is. What happened on that winter morning? "Disaster" or "Adventure" or "Danger" on a "Winter Morning" would all give us a hint of what is to come. Change "The Inn" to "The Inn of the Sixth Happiness," "The Haunted Inn," or "The Inn with the Secret Door" and we'll be tempted to read the story. "The Babysitter" becomes "The Elephant Babysitter," "The Cross-Eyed Babysitter," or "The Babysitter's Dilemma." And we want to know about "Dan's Journey Back to Life," "Dan's Incredible Journey," or "Dan's Nightmare Journey."

Be careful, though, to match your title to the mood of your memoir. Don't cheat. If you're writing a serious piece, give it a serious title. When you see "Out of Prison Darkness," "Not by Bread Alone," or "Divorce Is Not a Gentle Word," you expect to read something sober and thought-provoking. Titles like "Mountain Goats Never Say 'Cheese,'" "The Snake Has All the Lines," "There Are No Bathing Suits in Russia" signal that you are going to enjoy a laugh or at least something lighthearted. And "The Day the World Ended," "The Man Who Fell to Earth," or "The Plot to Steal a Fighter Plane" forecast drama and adventure.

No matter what the mood of your writing, be sure your title gives some idea of your subject. "Voyage by Bus" tells us at once we'll be reading about a bus trip. "January's Brittle Beauty" suggests scenes of icicles and snow on trees and houses, and "Come Ride the Space Shuttle" lets us know, of course, what it might be like to ride into space.

Sometimes a writer chooses a deceptive title without even realizing it. No doubt author Charles McGarry, who wrote a suspense novel called *The Secret Lovers,* thought it was a good title. Yet people who bought the book expected a racy romance filled with spicy sex scenes. To their disappointment, the secret lovers turned out to be spies and plotters who loved secrets.

It's generally best if your title is understandable and easy to pronounce. Some years ago when Solzhenitzyn's *Gulag Archipelago,* a lengthy epic of the horrors of Russian prison camps, first came on the market, one woman who plowed through it decided that a friend ought to read it too. When she mentioned the title, the friend, who had not heard of the book, said, "But I don't like travel stories." *Sieg Heil, Diaghilev,* and *Shiatsu* don't attract readers unless they happen to understand German, know who Diaghilev was, or are acquainted with oriental healing arts.

Be careful, though, when searching for a title that it doesn't tell too much. You don't want to give the story away. Would you read "The Arch Terrorist Who Went Scot Free," "Alone Across Alaska—I Made It," or "Kidnaped and Returned Alive"?

Publishers believe titles are so important that they often change them. Margaret Mitchell titled her great Civil War novel *Tomorrow Is Another Day*. Her publisher changed it to the now famous *Gone With the Wind*. Would it have become an enduring bestseller with the first title? Perhaps not. *Gone With the Wind* promises something exciting and intriguing. But who really cares that tomorrow is another day?

Though you may now be able to recognize a good title, how do you find one for your own writing?

You might begin by looking through your manuscript for a key word or phrase. One-word titles like *Earthquake, Caged, Jaws, Vertigo* have been popular. But they must be action words that give a good idea of your story, not just labels. Or you may find a phrase repeated over and over in your memoir. Writer Zoa Sherbourne chose the title *Almost April* for her first novel when she realized that those two words were repeated again and again. And the humorous title of Jean Kerr's book *The Snake Has All the Lines* comes from her young son's complaint. Given the part of Adam in a play about Adam and Eve, he protested, "But the snake has all the lines."

Sometimes you can create a good title by playing with words. Give a tired old cliché, a quotation, or a pun a new twist. Words and phrases that have been worn out with overuse can be revived by changing a word or two. "Back to Nurture," "A Bed of Neuroses," "Pandora's Book," and "Jill of All Trades" have a new sparkle.

The Los Angeles *Times* excels in pun titles. A story about a dog attending college with his master carried the headline "Bachelor of Arfs"; an account of a flea infestation "A Bad Year for Fleadom Fighters"; and a book review section "Balancing the Books."

Or you might like a musical title, one that repeats a
sound or a letter. "Tell-Tale Titles," *Wind in the Willows,*
"Meet Miss Marshall," all are easy to remember.

Once in a while you may want to ask a question in your
title and answer it in your writing. "How Did I Get to Be
Forty?" gives us a humorous response to that problem.
"Who Killed the Bog Men?" presents a historical question
that has really never been answered. And "Is It Worth the
Risk?" tells of mountain-climbing adventures and why the
climbers do it.

Some titles make a statement. But be careful. Like a
statement in your beginning or ending, it must be crisp,
to the point, and not too long. "We Owned the Sea,"
"Santa's Pack Held Thirty Toys," and "Here Be Dragons"
are all good statement titles. Each one makes us wonder
about who and where and why. And we'll read on to find
out.

And of course there's the topic title, perhaps the most
common of all. Yet it can be the dullest, for it's often just
a label. In writing about a dream, you're tempted to call
your memoir "A Dream." But we've all had dreams and
most of us would not be interested. Change it to "The
Gossamer Dream" and you have an intriguing title. Or
maybe you want to write about a special school you at-
tended, a converted chickenhouse. You could title it just
"The School," but, again, that's a label. Make it "The
Chickenhouse School" and we'll just have to read it.

But suppose you've tried and tried and just can't seem
to find any title that sounds right. What can you do?

Make a list. Write down every title you can think of no
matter how impossible it seems. Use words and ideas from
your memoir. Then read the list over. Maybe you can
combine parts of one title with another. Play with them.

Move words around. Perhaps you'll come up with a perfect title. In writing my memoir of an adventure in the South Seas, I tried a whole page of titles before I found one I liked: "Disaster in a Polynesian Wave," "The Biggest Wave," "Waves of Disaster," "Caught in a Polynesian Wave," "Threat in a Polynesian Wave," "Struck by a Wave of Disaster," "The Edge of Disaster," "Path to Disaster," "Caught in the Biggest Wave," "Wind and a Wave and a Boy," and, finally, "Peril in a Polynesian Wave."

Check titles in magazines and books, too. Use some of their strong, picture-making words but be original. Don't copy them exactly. "Mad, Marvelous Manhattan" could become "Mad, Marvelous Main Street." "The Secret Path to Peking" might be "The Secret Path" to anywhere. And "Darling, You Were Wonderful" could be changed to "Mother, You Were Wonderful" or some other name.

Look at magazine ads, too. Their writers are paid fabulous sums to think of words that will snap you to attention. How about "Wow! What a delicious surprise!" heading a steak-sauce ad? Just the word "Wow!" followed by almost anything will make us slide to a stop. A cake ad, "A White Christmas Should Have a Rainbow," could be changed to "A Rainbow Christmas" or another holiday with a rainbow feeling. And "Bouncin' and Behavin' Hair" might be just "Bouncin' and Behavin' " as a title for a childhood story of fun and pranks.

Don't forget newspaper headlines, either. News writers search for words that attract attention. "Arrest for Drugstore Robberies," "Budget Battlers Give Up," "Dope Probe in Crash," all have attention-getting words. Scan your newspaper to find ideas and words to use in your own titles.

Now, to practice, look through a favorite magazine.

Copy titles that especially appeal to you. Then change them for stories you might write. Look at the ads, too. Play with them. Twist and turn the words until they really reach out and grab you. Then go back to your memoir. Read it again and give it a billboard title that will make us all want to read on.

8

Show, Don't Tell

In your memoirs, we not only want to see the word picture you are painting. We also want to hear the sounds, taste the food, touch the cloth, smell the smoke. We want to share your sensations, not just read about them. Writer T. H. Watkins used all of his senses except touch to describe the town of Mendocino, California.

Time is slowed, urgency deteriorates, and life is expanded to include the smell of the sea-wind, the sound of a crowing rooster, the sight of a spavined white horse nibbling in a tiny pasture, the taste of flapjacks and coffee at the Sea Gull Inn.

From "A Rare and Special Place,"
California Living Magazine, April 6, 1975

A twelve-year-old boy, assigned to practice using his senses on the playground, responded with a poem.

I see a dragonfly, brittle, awaiting.
I see the leaves, dry, parched, lifeless.
I see papers, white, square, lonely.
I see a wire fence, mechanical, grasping, nonchalant.
I see lizards, sunbaked and quick.

I hear the wind, cool, inviting.
I hear eighth graders, demanding, independent.
I hear Mac, the janitor, hot in voice and work.

I feel gravel, coarse, gritty.
I feel flies, delicate, prickly.
I feel leaves, fresh, cold.

I smell trash, dirty, rotten.
I smell trees, each unique, wise.
I smell asphalt, hot, old, dirty.

                    Evan Wild

You too can use your senses to create vivid pictures. Searching through your memory box you find a snapshot of a mountain lake. A pine forest encircles it beneath snow-tipped peaks. You want to write about your camping trip to that lake. But the picture is flat. How can you show it in 3D?

Use detail. Be definite. You might write:

Dew hung on a cobweb in the sun.

That's not bad but it's not quite detailed enough.

Dew hung on a cobweb, each drop sparkling like a jewel in the sun.

Now we can see the dew on that cobweb.

A breeze blew across the lake.

What kind of breeze? And how did it blow?

A whisper of a breeze rippled across the lake.

In that sentence we find out it was a slight breeze. Next, we look at the mountain.

The tree-covered mountain rose steeply behind our tent.

What kind of trees? How steep was that mountain?

Pine trees climbed in almost vertical lines up the mountain behind our tent.

Besides detail, have you noticed the nouns in the revised sentences? They are like the easel you place your canvas on when painting a picture. They hold your writing up and give it strength. Use them instead of adjectives when you can.

"It's pretty cold out here," my father said.

Pretty doesn't say very much, does it?

"It must be down to twenty degrees out here," my father said.

Don't you almost shiver as you feel that cold?

A beautiful fish jumped in the lake.

What kind of fish? What did it really look like?

In the lake a rainbow trout jumped, its iridescence glinting in the sun.

That fish really does sound beautiful, now that we can see it.

The glowing fire felt warm on our half-frozen fingers.

The fire does feel warm, but you can make that feeling stronger.

We felt the glow of the fire, its warmth driving the chill from our half-frozen fingers.

Verbs as well as nouns can strengthen your word picture. They are the bold brush strokes that give life and action. Try to substitute verbs for adverbs.

I stopped abruptly, yelling fearfully as a bear came down the path.

We know you are afraid but do we feel your fear? Change *abruptly* and *fearfully* to strong verbs and see what happens.

I skidded to a stop, stiffened and let out a yell as a bear came down the path.

I'm ready to run, aren't you?
Try verbs instead of adverbs in this sentence.

As dawn slowly appeared, my father quickly opened the tent flap.

As dawn crept over the horizon, my father jumped up to flip the tent flap back.

Getting rid of *slowly* and *quickly*, we watch the dawn creep and father jump up.

Drowsily we got out of our sleeping bags and ran speedily down to the lake.

The adverbs *drowsily* and *speedily* don't help to make the picture clear.

We rubbed our eyes, unzipped our sleeping bags, and raced down to the lake.

With the strong verbs *rubbed, unzipped,* and *raced,* you don't need *drowsily* and *speedily* to show us what's happening.

Don't throw out all adverbs and adjectives, though. They're like salt in your soup. You need them for flavor, but use them sparingly.

And something else we like to see in any picture is color. Use it in your writing. Listen to this sentence.

The sunset faded as it sank behind the mountain.

I can't see this sunset, can you? Add color and see what happens.

The sunset, a kaleidoscope of purple, red, and orange, faded as the sun sank behind the mountain.

See how vivid that sunset is now?

Clumps of wild iris grew beneath the pines.

We know pines are green, but if you've never seen wild iris, they're only black print on white paper.

Clumps of wild iris, in shades of deep purple, pale lavender, and white, grew beneath the pines.

See how adding color brightens the picture?

I could see the hunter's cap bobbing in and out among the trees.

What color is a hunter's cap? And we assume the trees were green. But were they?

I could see the bright red hunter's cap bobbing among the aspens wearing their fall shades of orange and gold.

Besides looking at your picture, we want to hear how things sound. We respond in one way or another to the blare of rock music, the throb of marching drums, or the slow rhythm of a waltz. Sounds can be harsh and irritating or pleasant and relaxing. The cheerful chirping of crickets, the noon blast of a factory whistle, or the monotonous drip of water can help us hear as well as see the story you're writing.

What do you hear in this sentence?

My daughter sat up in bed as she heard the ambulance in the street.

If your imagination is active enough, you may imagine the sound of the ambulance. But you can't definitely hear anything. Listen again.

My daughter sat up in bed as the shrill siren of the ambulance shattered the silence of the street.

Now the siren is a clear sound, isn't it? Here's another noise you often hear. Yet, no matter how much you hate it, you don't hear it in this sentence.

On Saturday mornings I awoke to the sound of lawn mowers cutting the grass.

Revise it something like this:

On Saturday mornings I groaned awake to the sound of lawn mowers chattering back and forth across the grass.

I groan, the mowers chatter, and you hear them.
    And look at this sentence. What do you really hear?

The dog growled as my husband opened the gate.

Was it a loud growl? Threatening? Fierce? Revise it.

A growl rumbled up from deep in the dog's throat as my husband opened the gate.

Now I'd back off, wouldn't you?
    Not only do we like to see and hear, we like to touch, to find out how something feels. When you shop for a coat or a suit, don't you touch the cloth as well as look at it? Is it soft, firm, smooth, rough? Let us feel the wool or fur, the cold hands, sharp needle, or wet sand if they are in your story.

You might write:

His hands are cold.

How cold? Slightly or freezing?

His hands are like chunks of cold marble.

Now we shiver as we touch them.

I could feel the needle prick my finger.

You can feel this needle but I'm not sure we can.

I could feel the needle, stiletto sharp, stab into my finger.

Ouch! We share that stab.

The sand felt wet.

How does wet sand feel? Packed down and hard? Or soft and squishy?

The sand felt like soggy cardboard.

We know soggy cardboard isn't hard. It's spongy.

One of the most neglected senses in our writing is our sense of taste. Yet our taste buds readily respond to stimulation. The four primary tastes are salty, bitter, sweet, and sour. But you can add variations, such as grainy, hot, cool, peppery, smooth, tangy, tart, rancid, caustic. Though we usually think of this sense in relation to food, we react to many other tastes. Air, dust, mildew, perfume, insecticides are a few.

When you want us to really taste something, be specific. Name the sensation exactly.

They could taste the sea air.

What if you've never been near the sea? This is too indefinite.

They could taste the salt in the sea air.

This lets us know just how that air tastes.

My sister tried to spit out the taste of the olive she had just picked from the tree.

What is this taste? Sour, rancid, rotten?

My sister tried to spit out the bitterness of the olive she had just picked from the tree.

Few people know how bitter olives are before they are processed but this gives us some idea.

I could taste the dust settling in layers over the room.

We've all tasted dust swirling up from a road or a floor. But how can we share that taste?

My mouth felt dry and hot from the taste of dust settling over the room.

Tasting, touching, hearing, seeing can all add to your stories. Yet the sense of smell often sharpens a memory more readily. Some experiences are linked forever with special odors. To me, the first lilacs will always mean spring no matter where I live. When I was growing up in Colorado, the smell of lilacs signaled that it was time to take off long stockings and winter underwear. To you it might have meant getting out the jump rope and jacks or the baseball bat.

Just as you do when sharing the other senses, when sharing the sense of smell, tell us exactly what it is.

My nose twitched at the smell of fire and burning wood.

How do fire and burning wood smell?

My nose twitched at the smell of smoke and burning pine.

Isn't the smell stronger, now? And don't you want to find out if it means a pleasant campfire or a crackling forest fire?

Sometimes unpleasant odors remain longer in your memory than those you like.

The old boat smelled bad.

You probably won't forget this old boat but *bad* really doesn't mean anything to us. Shakespeare, in *The Tempest,* mentions "a very ancient and fish-like smell." You might adapt that to your old boat.

The old boat smelled of mildew and dying fish.

The words *mildew* and *dying fish* are so strong they almost wrinkle your nose.

And don't forget those kitchen odors. Sometimes they are the strongest of all in our memories. Fresh-baked bread, pickles in the crock, garlic in the spaghetti sauce are some of my favorites. And how about pies?

The kitchen smelled of apple pies baking in the oven.

Remember how those pies smelled? Let us smell them, too.

The sweet, spicy smell of apple pies baking in the oven filled the kitchen.

Besides sharing your senses, use comparisons to show us your picture. Similes and metaphors describe one thing as something else. You may remember that you call comparisons similes when you join them by *like* or *as.* They are as old as speech itself. Our earliest ancestors probably used expressions like "sharp as a tiger's tooth," "mad as a hornet," "hungry as a bear." And you'll find similes throughout the Old Testament. "Sharp as a two-edged sword," "bitter as wormwood," "still as a stone" are only a few. Some you might write could be:

We could hear a tree scratching its branches like fingernails against the window.

The fog, like a pale gray curtain, wrapped around us.

Grass like green fringe bordered the creek.

When you leave out *like* or *as* and say directly that one thing is something else, you call it a metaphor.

We could hear a tree scratching its fingernails against the window.

The fog, a pale gray curtain, wrapped around us.

A fringe of green grass bordered the creek.

You do have to be careful with comparisons, though. Always make them appropriate to the picture you are creating. Former Secretary of State Alexander Haig was a master at mixing metaphors. He often used expressions like "I don't want to saddle myself with a statistical fence."

Even though you have a super-vivid imagination, you would find it hard to picture a fence as a saddle. To make his statement clear, he could have said, "I don't want to surround myself with a statistical fence."

A student wrote:

Tons of perspiration flowed down her cheeks as she bent over the volcano of a stove.

We think of tons of coal or grain or cement, not perspiration. And is the stove about to erupt like a volcano? Revise the comparison.

Rivulets of perspiration flowed down her cheeks as she bent over the inferno of a stove.

The revision makes the comparison logical, and we can feel the heat in the room without being confused.

It's time, now, to see how well you can use your senses and create comparisons. Try the same experiment as the boy who wrote the poem. Look at the garden or the street or around the room. What do you see? Write it down. Close your eyes. What do you hear, feel, taste, smell? Add it all to your list. How many senses could you use? As you write this week, try to use them all, showing rather than telling.

For more practice, write a sentence about each of the following to show rather than tell.

1. What you see when caught out in a violent storm
2. The smell of honeysuckle on a hot, humid afternoon
3. The taste of an apple, or cod liver oil, or swirling dust
4. The sound of glass breaking in the kitchen, or of a fist against flesh
5. The feel of gravel under bare feet

Use similes and metaphors to compare each of these to something else.

1. A lawn in spring
2. A tall, thin teenage boy
3. A dripping water tap
4. A bowl of popcorn
5. A summer afternoon

9

Flash Back, Move Forward

In reading over the memoir you've just written, you suddenly realize you've left out something that happened before your story began. Your reader needs to know about it to understand. What can you do?

Use a flashback.

A flashback interrupts a story to give important information about the past. It may be an entire piece or only a few paragraphs. When the whole story flashes back, a present experience usually triggers the memory. A forest scene reminded one student of a special picnic.

When I pass through a forest with certain kinds of trees and lush green ferns, the tumblers of my mind click back to our "primordial adventure" the year when I was eight.

Her story continues in a flashback of an exciting picnic on a mountain lot in the redwoods. At the end she returns to the present.

The tumblers click. The time warp vanishes, as the lot soon did, replaced by something new, as was our adventure.

From "Primordial Adventure," by Louise Mohr,
Silhouettes of the Past

Some of your memoirs will be like this, written entirely in a flashback. But often you may wish to start your story

with an intensely exciting incident to capture our interest. Then you have to flash back to give us information we
need to know in order to understand what's happening.
In a story, "The Love Cards," I began this way:

Creak-crack-creak. I sat up in bed. Creak-crack-creak. The
sound came again. What was it? Footsteps in the hall?

Of course not, I thought, flicking on the light. It had to be the
hardwood boards in the floor contracting in the cool summer
night. I looked at the clock—2:00 A.M.

Flashback begins:

Only eight hours since I'd left my husband at the airport, but
now it seemed like eight years. He'd be gone two weeks attending a Bible study course in Wisconsin. He'd been gone before
but I had always stayed with friends or my daughter.

This time I had chosen to stay home. The big garden had to
be watered, the fruit and vegetables canned and frozen. Besides, I was a little ashamed. Why couldn't a mature woman
conquer her fear of noises in the night?

Return to the story:

In the morning, I dragged about my work without enthusiasm. I had plenty to do, yet how many more sleepless nights
could I survive?

> "The Love Cards" by Fanny-Maude Evans,
> *Guideposts Magazine,* March, 1982

Sometimes a flashback needs to be long to give us
enough information.

It was the first day of school at District No. 3 in Nebraska.
Grabbing his lunch pail, the last pupil ran screaming down the
hill after the others. I sank with a weary sigh into my chair. "It's
impossible. I can't teach thirty-six pupils and all eight grades,"
I moaned. The day had been utter chaos.

Flashback begins:

I recalled my enthusiasm when I had come a few days early

to the Scheurich home where I was going to room, in order to prepare for that first day of school. Lou, the twenty-three-year-old son, had taken me to the little white school building on the hill while he went to Hoskins, two miles away. I felt a thrill of excitement when I turned the key to my own school. Ever since I was a child, I had planned some day to be a teacher. When I was a senior in high school, I taught the second grade for three weeks while the teacher was ill. At Teacher's College that summer, I took courses in rural school methods and observed the model school with twelve pupils. But I had never been in a real rural school.

That morning, when I entered the building, a musty smell greeted me. The floor was strewn with dead leaves and dried mud. A small cupboard, about three feet high, held a few soiled, torn books. On top I could see a tin water pail and a long-handled dipper. "Ugh!" I thought. "That will have to go."

Double seats for older pupils occupied the back of the room on the right side with smaller ones in front. Those for the little ones were on the left. Small blackboards were placed between the windows. The teacher's desk stood on a raised platform in front flanked by a pump organ on one side and a potbellied stove on the other.

I opened the teacher's desk and let out a scream. There, in one corner, a chewed-up American flag formed a mouse nest. It held five hairless baby mice. Since there was no one around to see me, I carried the drawer outside and carefully placed the nest by the coal shed. I wondered if the mother ever found her babies.

The next day, Ann, the daughter where I lived, and I came laden with scrub pails, soap and rags. We heated water on the stove and scrubbed the floor on our hands and knees and washed the desks and windows. Little did I dream when I signed the contract for $55 a month that I would have to be a janitor also. I, who had never started a fire in my life.

Return to the story:

Now, I sat with my head drooping like the wilted goldenrod and yellow sunflowers.

> From "First Day of School in 1917" by Leona Cox,
> *Silhouettes of the Past*

Generally it's wise to make a flashback shorter unless, like this one, it's filled with interesting facts we need to know. If the flashback is too long, you risk losing your reader, especially if you are interrupting exciting action.

Sometimes you need a flashback to explain how the past is influencing the present, as I did in this story.

I didn't look forward to my fortieth birthday. Somehow it seemed that from then on everything would be downhill. But just before that dreaded date, four words changed my whole life.

Flashback begins:

My daughter had just graduated from high school and won a scholarship to a major college. And my husband had won a grant to study at a top technical school. Intending to be funny, a friend turned to me and asked, "What have you won?"

The words seared into my mind for days. What had I won? There were certainly no prizes for thousands of home-cooked meals, tons of dishes washed and endless baskets of mending. Still, raising a daughter to be a responsible citizen and encouraging a husband in his career climb should be enough. But was it?

Return to the story:

On the day my daughter left for college, I sat down to do some serious thinking.

> "Second Half, Second Chance" by Fanny-Maude Evans
> *Lutheran Women*, April, 1979

Notice that these flashbacks flow with the story. You hardly notice that they are interruptions. How can you lead into your flashback so smoothly?

One way is to use a key word.

"Leukemia," Don said. "That's the diagnosis."
Flashback:
Leukemia! Waves of shock poured over me. Leukemia. Don
had it. Just like his father. And his brother. They'd both died of
leukemia.
Return to the story:
I looked up at my husband. "You'll beat it, Don," I said. "We'll
beat it together."

Sometimes you can use a question. This piece begins
with action and a question. Then the whole story is a
flashback of a disastrous year.

Crumpling the sheet of yellow paper, I hurled it across the
room. A hard knot of anger pulled across my stomach. How
could I ever write our Christmas letter updating friends and
relatives on the past year?
Flashback:
It just wasn't fair! The whole year had been nothing but
trouble.

The story continues in the flashback to explain why the
writer couldn't write the letter. Near the end, she realizes
the misfortunes of the year had really, in a sense, been
blessings. The flashback ends, and the story:

Grabbing my pencil I started to write a very special Christmas letter.

"The Christmas Letter" by Fanny-Maude Evans,
Family Life Today, December, 1978

A shock statement is a good way to introduce a flashback, too.

He couldn't mean what he'd just said!

Flashback:

Why, she'd waited ten years to go on this trip. She'd worked and saved and planned. Now he wanted to cancel it.

Return to story:

"I'll go by myself," she yelled. "You'll see."

Dramatic action can also lead into a flashback. It doesn't have to be a physical or emotional upheaval. It can be as simple as an argument with a spouse or child or with a maid.

Something was wrong with Rosa. When she brought in the breakfast tray she set it down so hard that the cups danced in their saucers and the strong Brazilian coffee spilled onto the table.

"What's the matter with her?" my husband asked, reaching for the pitcher of warm milk to dilute his coffee.

I sighed. "I don't know. I certainly hope she's not going to start being temperamental."

Flashback:

Rosa was the last of a long line of maids who had stopped at my gate asking for work. When I first joined my husband in São Paulo, Brazil, where he had been assigned to the military school, I had hired one of the girls. She was so ignorant and inefficient that I decided to struggle alone with the problems of establishing a home. Yet my limited knowledge of Brazilian customs had made life quite difficult until Rosa arrived. Older than most of the girls, she seemed so strong and capable that I decided to try her. Except for minor disagreements I had been highly pleased until this morning.

Return to story:

When I finished my breakfast I went to the kitchen.

By now, you may realize that there are certain types of words that introduce a flashback. *Remember, thought, recalled, back when, then, in that year, flashed through my mind, some years ago* are a few.

Ending your flashback, you return to your story with words like *today, these days, times change, later.* A definite date or time of day can also be used to begin or end.

Another way to get into or out of a flashback is simply to set it off by leaving a space. In a flashback story about starting to school, the author could do it this way.

My revolt against starting school became my mother's and grandmother's favorite anecdote for many years. They always laughed while telling it and enjoyed remembering my absurd behavior. Never once did they recognize the chaotic condition of my mind as I faced that first day of school. First day? It took five days to get me to stay there.

Flashback begins:

Utter terror had gripped me as I tried desperately to hold onto the resolve I had secretly made to myself, "I'll never go to that school—not ever."

The writer continues with the daring and ingenious ways she used to try to stay away from school. She ends the flashback this way:

As old Maude took us home after two o'clock, I knew Mama and Grandma had won and I had lost.

Return to the present:

Today I know no member of my family ever recognized the incidents of those five days as a serious crisis in my childhood life. No passage of time can erase the terrifying trauma I felt, however. It will always remain indelibly etched on my own mind.

> "Revolt Against Starting School" by Ferol Slotte,
> *Silhouettes of the Past*

Though leaving space is easy, don't use the device often. Too many extra spaces can break up your story.

Some writers try to avoid flashbacks altogether. They

feel that they slow the story too much. Yet, when you have an anecdote or incident that will make a snappy, exciting beginning, use it, followed by a flashback to give necessary information. Or, if something you see or hear recalls a special memory, write your entire story as a flashback. After all, a memoir really is a flash back into the past.

For practice, write a memoir of a picnic, party, or adventure you remember vividly. Begin with an exciting incident, then flash back to give background information. Or write a complete story as a flashback.

10
Vigorous Verbs

Use strong verbs. You've heard this before. But why? And what makes a verb strong?

If you studied Latin, you'll probably never forget Julius Caesar's famous words "I came, I saw, I conquered." Those verbs have survived for hundreds of years because they have power. Yours can have power, too, if you make them strong.

The verb is the most important word in your sentence. It expresses action of persons or things:

Many people *play* tennis.
The town *overlooks* the lake.
Roses *are* my favorite flowers.

A lively verb gives your sentence vivid meaning.

Ron's fist *hit* the policeman's jaw.

Hit is not really the weakest verb, but you can do better. Try any of these:

Ron's fist *smashed, battered, slammed into,* or *rammed* the policeman's jaw.

Can't you feel that blow now?

Verbs have two voices, active and passive. William Zinsser, in *On Writing Well,* says, "Use active verbs unless there is no comfortable way to get around using a passive verb. The difference between an active-verb style and a passive-verb style, in pace, clarity and vigor, is the difference between life and death for a writer."

Since you want your verbs to live, make them active. Active verbs push your sentence forward. Something or someone does something and words are in normal order.

The new student *read* the theme.

The verb *read* is active, for the student does the acting. But watch out! Passive verbs can creep in without your realizing it. Some of you have the habit of using them. Break that habit! Passive verbs are just that—passive. They give your sentence only a slight push. You turn the word order around and the action is done by something or someone.

The theme *was read* by the new student.

See how the whole sentence is reversed? It is longer, too, and it is weak and indirect.

Don't throw out all passive verbs, though. Sometimes you need them. If you don't know who is doing something, use the passive voice.

The hall was built in 1927.
More men than women are elected to the legislature.
The houses were all sold last week.

Here we don't know who built the hall, who elected more men, or who sold the houses, and we use the passive voice.

Also, if the person doing the acting is not important to the thought of the sentence, you can use a passive verb.

After the tour, the princess was driven to the airport.

We don't care and probably don't know who drove her.

He was given the medal because he risked his life to rescue the girl.

Here the medal and the reason for it are important, not who awarded it.

After the storm, the pool was thoroughly cleaned.

Who cleaned the pool doesn't matter. We just want to be sure it is clean before we dive in.

Watch out, too, for the preposition *by*. You've probably noticed that it follows many passive verbs.

It was late when the gift was received by us.
The new dress was admired by the girl.
A red roadster was desired by our family.

Leave *by* out and turn these sentences around.

It was late when we received the gift.
The girl admired the new dress.
Our family desired a red roadster.

When you cross out *by* and make your verbs active, see how much more forceful they are?

Bring your writing alive, too, by checking your use of the verb *to be*. Its various forms—*is, are, was, were, shall be, will be, been*—are weak and don't go anywhere. Yet it's almost impossible to write three sentences without them. Substitute action verbs when you can.

It *was* not known when the volcano would erupt.
No one knew when the volcano would erupt.

They *were* afraid of lightning.
They shook all over when lightning flashed.

He *is* the fastest runner on the team.
He outruns every other member of the team.

See how your verbs come alive when you take out *was,
were,* and *is?*

To study strong verbs, notice those in newspaper headlines. They shout at you to attract attention.

Slashes in Spending *Force* School Cutbacks
Man *Trapped* for Seven Days in Wrecked Car
Youth Leader *Steals* the Show
Group *Barred* from Parade
Hundreds *Stranded* in Blizzard

You can feel the power in these verbs, can't you?
Look at magazine ads, too. They say STOP! LOOK!

Discover Heavenly Comfort
Flaunt Your True Colors With Colorfast
Cover Girl *Cares*
Save a Lettuce's Life
Reach Out and *Touch* Someone

You might list the verbs you find most powerful. Then
go back and read your own writing over. If some sentences don't sound quite right, look at your verbs. See if
you can substitute some from the list you've made. Then
change passive to active voice if you can. Circle *is, was,
were,* and other forms of *to be.* Change as many as possible to vigorous verbs that go somewhere. For practice, use
strong verbs in these sentences. Change passive to active
when possible.

1. Because of the storm the hike was canceled by us.
2. The accident at the corner was seen by Mr. Smith.
3. The report has been finished by them.

4. He said the book was given to him.
5. The notebook I lost has been returned by Sam.

Try to replace forms of *to be* with action verbs in these sentences. Rewrite, if necessary, but remember you often must use *is, was, were* forms.

1. Their methods are up-to-date.
2. There is nothing we can do about it.
3. That store is open at 9.00 A.M.
4. Mary is seriously ill.
5. The dog was barking all night.

11

How to Keep Your Reader Awake

The other day at the library, a friend told me she'd like to write about her life.

"Why don't you, then?" I asked.

"Oh, nothing really exciting ever happened to me. How would I keep my readers awake?"

I laughed. "There are ways," I told her. "You just have to know what they are."

Are you wondering, too, how to make your memoirs so exciting and interesting your readers will stay awake?

First of all, you have to use suspense. Keep us wondering what's going to happen next. The Japanese do this in their gardens. They design the paths with many curves and corners to hide what's ahead. They hope you'll be so curious you'll walk on to find out.

In your story, to make us curious, start with a problem. It doesn't have to be life threatening. You don't need to find a body in your closet or stand at the edge of a crumbling cliff. Your problem can be as simple as the first time you visited a large city alone. Like this student's:

July, vacation time, 1918, with World War I still raging, seemed hardly the time to go to New York City. But my friend Evelyn's husband could not get a furlough, and we decided to visit him.

Evelyn, aged seventeen, and I, twenty years old, in our inno-
cence thought we would have no trouble finding a room. Off we
went on the old steam railway, burdened with a straw suitcase
that held clothes for a two-day stay.

We'll never forget our arrival in New York. Such confusion!

"Innocents Abroad in New York" by Rozilla M. Reed,
Silhouettes of the Past

What happened? Did they find a room? Don't you want
to know?

Keep your reader guessing. Don't solve your problem
immediately. In the story "The Love Cards," the problem
is the mystery of who sent the cards when the writer was
fearful of staying alone.

In the mail that day there was a single postcard. When I
turned it over I read a handlettered message:

As the candle,
    Lights up the darkness
So shall my darkness
    Be lighted by Him.

No name, no clue as to who had sent it. Just the impersonal "U.
S. Postal Service."

Who would send such a message? Who, besides a few friends
and my daughter, knew about my fears?

The next morning there was another card. This time, two
birds in flight had been pasted beside a verse. Again there was
no signature, no clue.

See how such a simple problem can create suspense?
Not until almost the end of the story do you find out who
was sending the cards.

Pile the problems up, too. If you solve one, present

another. In this student's story about trying to escape from two rough men, she does this well.

I had walked several blocks when I heard this car coming along the street I was approaching. It turned the corner, and I saw that it was the old Ford roadster.

"There she is!" a man cried.

I was numb with terror but my long legs automatically started running. Fortunately the roadster had to turn around to go in the direction I was headed. I beat it crossing the street. Not burdened with a coat nor my books I had left in my classroom, I ran like a deer. I heard the car drawing near the curb behind me and the door open.

"We've got her now," said another voice.

"Yeh, boy. Stop!" his companion yelled.

Frantically I dashed deep into the wide lawn and close to the house I was passing. I flew across that yard to the next house and on to the next and the next and the next.

Seeing me running so near the buildings, the men seemed afraid to make a move. The rider kept opening his door wide to watch my progress.

I came to the end of that block and ran around the corner house. It was a relief to see that the lawns on this new street were also open. Some yards had dividing flower beds I dashed through. The men were swearing and laughing at my plight.

"We'll catch her at the next corner," I heard the driver say.

> "The Night Hunters" by Marjorie Heilbron,
> *Silhouettes of the Past*

The situation gets worse and worse. How can the girl escape? You can't put the story down until you find out.

To keep suspense rising, ask a question once in a while. Questions arouse your curiosity. You'll keep looking for the answer. In "The Magic Map," telling about an experience in Bremen, I use questions this way:

Back at the square once more, we parked in a no parking zone and pulled out our map.

Almost as if he had been waiting for us, a policeman popped up beside the car. We shuddered. What was the penalty in Germany for illegal parking? A ticket and a fine? Or jail? And what were German jails like?

"The Magic Map" Fanny-Maude Evans,
Odyssey, March-April, 1981.

Right away you ask your own questions. Did they get a ticket? What was the penalty? Did they really have to go to jail?

Sometimes you can keep us guessing by hinting at something that's going to happen. You forecast, not tomorrow's weather, but what's ahead in your memoir.

One writer began a story about a fierce bull by giving us just such a hint.

Over the years I'd prided myself on my ability to make friends with animals. Nicodemus, my grandfather's new Guernsey bull, was no exception even though Grandpa warned me, "Be careful! He's no plaything."

"The Old Nic" by Doris Bona,
Silhouettes of the Past

That warning tells you at once there's danger ahead. And you want to know what it is.

In some stories you can use time to create suspense. You have a problem to solve but there aren't enough minutes, hours, or days to do it. The story about a cruise in the South Seas uses the time element.

"Blast the luck!" The captain sank abruptly onto the gunwale of the disabled boat. He stared out at the waves.

"It's the devil of a long swim. We'd never make it."

He squinted at the green crescent ringing the village. "No way through that jungle. And this kid's foot can't wait. Coral cuts can be deadly."

Time can be just as important in an everyday story. Perhaps you remember a year when your daughter was to be the prom queen's attendant. Frantically you worked on her dress. On the evening of the prom you trimmed the last seam. But you snipped it too close. The whole bodice ripped out. In just one hour her date would arrive. What did you do?

Or your wife was in labor with your first child. Rushing her to the hospital miles away, you forgot about your leaking radiator. Your car overheated and stalled on a deserted road.

Readers won't put these stories down until they see how you solved your time problems.

Besides creating different kinds of problems, there is something else you can do to increase suspense. Change your pace.

Perhaps you've been presenting problems one after the other so fast that you're getting out of breath. You want to slow down. Or maybe you've been so slow and deliberate that each problem seems to take forever to solve. You're getting tired of them.

Remember how you feel at a concert, listening to soft, slow selections played one after the other. Before long you lose interest and begin to nod. Abruptly the violins and trumpets and drums change their tempo. They play faster and louder. You snap awake to listen once more.

So it is with your writing. Too much dialogue, narrative, or description all at once is tiresome. As in music, you must speed up and slow down. How can you do this?

To speed up you can show thoughts through dialogue and action rather than telling them.

Bill watched steam rise from the tub. Warily he dipped a finger in.

"Wow!" He jerked it back. "Hot as a volcano!"

"Be careful," I warned. "I've heard it's so hot it can give you a heart attack."

To slow down, tell us rather than show us what people are thinking.

Steam rose from the tub. Bill thought it looked hot as a volcano. He wondered if he would even dare to stick a finger in.

He tried it and jerked back.

I warned him to be careful. I'd heard that such hot water could give a person a heart attack.

To move your story faster, let us taste, touch, smell, hear, and see what's happening. This paragraph in the South Seas story goes fast.

"I'm thirsty," Rick grumbled, wrinkling his nose at the fishy smell of the beach.

"Get back!" Trev yelled, grabbing the boy. "You wanta drink salt water? I'll get you a green coconut. That'll give you some zip."

Now, to slow down, tell us rather than showing us what's happening.

Rick grumbled that he was thirsty. He wrinkled his nose at the fishy smell of the beach.

Suddenly Trev grabbed at him. He yelled that he was too near the waves, unless he wanted to drink salt water. He promised to get him a green coconut to give him some zip.

And do be careful with description. In the 1800s, people had plenty of time to gather around the fireplace in the evenings and read. They seemed to enjoy page after page of long descriptions. Today, we don't have that much time and want to get on with the story. Of course you need some description, but use it carefully. To speed up your writing, break it into short paragraphs. Interrupt it with dialogue, as in this scene along the road in the interior of Brazil.

We came to a small cemetery gaily decorated with paper flower wreaths in rainbow colors. A grinning mulatto workman looked up and waved his paintbrush at us.

"Mother, what's he doing?" My daughter, Dixie, asked. "Is he painting the tombstones?"

"Looks like it, doesn't it?" I said. "I think, though, he's probably using whitewash."

People strolled down the road from all directions bearing more of the paper wreaths. For this was the day before the annual memorial of the dead. Everyone was honoring departed friends and relatives with a paper decoration.

"Why don't they use real flowers?" Dixie asked.

"I don't know," was all I could say. It did seem odd. Why, in this land where so many exotic orchids grew on jungle trees, would anyone prefer flowers made of paper?

To slow your description, use longer paragraphs, less dialogue.

We came to a small cemetery gaily decorated with flower wreaths in rainbow colors. A grinning mulatto workman looked up and waved his paintbrush at us. My daughter, Dixie, wondered what he was doing.

"Is he painting the tombstones?" she asked. I told her it did look like it but he was probably just using whitewash.

People strolled down the road from all directions bearing

more of the paper wreaths. For this was the day before the annual memorial of the dead. Everyone was honoring departed friends and relatives with a paper decoration.

Dixie asked why they didn't use real flowers. I didn't know. It did seem odd, I thought, that in this land where so many exotic orchids grew on jungle trees people would prefer flowers made of paper.

In writing dialogue, to speed up the pace, use short paragraphs with little interruption by action, as I did in a conversation with a Brazilian maid.

"Rosa, why do you slam doors and bang the dishes on this beautiful morning?" I asked.

"Perhaps to the senhora the morning is beautiful," she snapped. "The senhora is rich and has a grand house and fine clothes."

"What do you mean?" I asked. "I am certainly not rich. My house is not grand. And my clothes are surely ordinary. Besides, even if this were true, what does it have to do with you? I do not understand."

"No, the senhora does not understand, and I, Rosa, do not understand. Why must I pass my days in hard work? Why do I not have the money, the dresses, the shoes?"

To slow dialogue down, interrupt conversations with action or thought. Use longer paragraphs.

"Rosa, why do you slam the doors and bang the dishes on this beautiful morning?" I asked, frowning. She was being impossible. Would I have to start searching for another maid?

She half-turned from washing vegetables at the sink. "Perhaps to the senhora the morning is beautiful." She scowled at me. "The senhora is rich and has a house and fine clothes." She turned back to the sink, splashing the water as she thumped the celery and lettuce down on the drain.

I looked at her. What did she mean? Certainly by Brazilian

standards I wasn't rich. And our house was not grand. It was no "palacete" as the Brazilians call their magnificent mansions. I had no personal hairdresser, either, or a manicurist or dressmaker or tailor who came at my bidding. Yet, perhaps to Rosa, raised in the ghetto, I did seem rich. But why, suddenly, had this become a problem?

"Rosa," I said, raising my voice, for with her back turned I was not sure she would hear me. "Even if I were rich, what does this have to do with you? I do not understand."

She banged a pan down on the counter. "No, the senhora does not understand. And I do not understand. Why must I pass my days in hard work? Why do I not have the money, the dresses, the shoes?"

Above all, to keep your reader awake, be an artist, not a photographer. Choose the most important scenes, incidents, and details to include in your story. Sometimes you're tempted to tell everything you remember when much of it has little to do with your tale. In this story about a disappearing aunt the writer needed to learn what to leave out.

We boarded the train in San Francisco and crossed the Sierras. We went through Nevada, Utah, Wyoming, and the northern part of Colorado. Finally, we reached Denver and got off at Union Station. But we couldn't find my aunt anywhere.

What interests you in this paragraph? It's the last line, about the aunt, isn't it? Rewritten, it reads like this:

In San Francisco we boarded the train to Denver. But, when we finally arrived at Union Station, we couldn't find my aunt anywhere.

Now you're interested. You want to know where the aunt was, what happened to her.

Be careful with detailed action, too. Leave out everything that doesn't directly concern your story. Who really cares what you ate for breakfast unless it was poisoned? And do you have to tell us that you undressed, washed your face, and brushed your teeth before you crawled into bed? Use words like *the next morning, in the afternoon, afterward,* to skip over watching TV, having dinner, going to bed, unless, like the poisoned breakfast, it's important to your piece.

I condensed years of moving that had little to do with my story into one paragraph.

"Moving on" was our motto. I spent hours and days and weeks searching for a house or apartment, packing and unpacking. Even when our baby daughter arrived, nothing changed. We went right on moving from one town to another, to different states, and, finally, to Brazil.

See how you can skip through years of moving, across thousands of miles, and finally to Brazil in a few words?

Let's see, now, what you can do to keep us awake. Choose an exciting or frightening experience. It can be as ordinary as the first meal you cooked for your in-laws, the day you took your first driver's test, or that time, as a tot, when you wandered away from your mother in the shopping center.

Remember to pile on the problems until the final crisis when you are ready to solve everything. If your story is long, add more problems. If it's short, use only a few. Leave out all unimportant details. Change your pace now and then. If you do these things, you won't need to worry about your reader going to sleep.

12

To Repeat or Not to Repeat

In the last chapter you learned how to keep your reader awake. There's something else you need to know, now, to keep us from dozing. You need to know when repetition is good and when it is bad.

Do you have a friend who talks like this? "Well, see, we went on this trip. The whole thing was a disaster, see? The ship didn't have good stabilizers. See, it rolled so much we were awful sick. And when we got to the island, see, the hotel didn't have rooms for us."

By now you don't want to hear or "see" any more of your friend's story. That one word *see* has ruined what could have been a good tale.

Certain words seem to latch onto all of us without our realizing it. They crop up again and again, killing any interest in what we're saying.

So it is with your writing. Repetition that creeps in unintentionally can dull the most exciting story. One writer discovered he had used the word *very* more than 650 times in a novel he wrote. I have a problem with the little word *too* in my own writing. Some years ago I handed a manuscript to a friend to criticize. When she gave it back she said, "I loved the story except for one thing. Too many *too*'s."

She was right. When I checked, I found *too*'s sprouting like weeds on every page.

How can you avoid this kind of unconscious repetition?

You have to listen to your writing. Read it aloud or tape it and play it back. Words and phrases you've repeated will pop out like jacks-in-the-box. One student wrote this sentence:

In the book, the final chapter of the book tells what happens to the heroine of the book.

When she read it to the class she could hardly believe she had written *book* so often.

Is all repetition bad, though? What about this, written by reporter Pete Hamill when the hostages were returning from Iran? A woman with a yellow ribbon pinned to her coat told him,

"I saw them coming home, and the first night, on TV, I started to cry. And then every night after that, I cried. I cried when they got to Algeria and I cried when they got to Germany and I cried when they got to Washington. And I know I'm gonna cry today. And I won't be ashamed of myself."

San Francisco *Chronicle,* January 31, 1981

Can't you see this woman crying and crying and crying? If she'd just said she cried, without repeating the word, we wouldn't have shared her feelings nearly so vividly.

To hit a word hard, repeat it. Writers throughout the ages have done this. Notice the repetition in this short paragraph written by Samuel Johnson.

I am very fond of the company of ladies. I like their beauty, I like their delicacy, I like their vivacity and I like their silence.

And you like the way he used that word, don't you?

Poets know how to use repetition effectively, too. Edgar Allan Poe in his long poem "The Raven" repeated words and phrases in each stanza.

Once upon a midnight dreary, while I pondered, weak and
  weary,
Over many a quaint and curious volume of forgotten lore,
While I nodded, nearly napping, suddenly there came a
  tapping,
As of someone gently *rapping, rapping at my chamber door*:
" 'Tis some visitor," I muttered, "*tapping at my chamber
  door:*
    Only this and *nothing more."*

Ah, distinctly I remember it was in the bleak December,
And each separate dying ember wrought its ghost upon the
  floor.
Eagerly I wished the morrow;—vainly I had sought to
  borrow
From my books surcease of *sorrow—sorrow* for the lost
  Lenore,
For the rare and radiant maiden whom the angels name
  Lenore,
    Nameless here for evermore.

And the silken sad uncertain rustling of each purple curtain
Thrilled me—filled me with fantastic terrors never felt
  before;
So that now, to still the beating of my heart, I stood
  repeating,
"'Tis some visitor entreating entrance *at my chamber door*—
Some late visitor entreating entrance *at my chamber door:*
    This it is *and nothing more."*

Poe ends four more stanzas with the words *and nothing
more.* Then he changes to *nevermore* to end the remain-
ing stanzas.

And have you noticed how songwriters often repeat
words for emphasis? Remember when we used to sing

"Home Sweet Home" at the end of a party or get-together?

Home, home, sweet, sweet home!
There's no place like home! There's no place like home!

John Howard Payne

There was no doubt how we felt about home as we repeated these two lines at the end of each verse.

Even though you're not a poet or a songwriter, you can use the same technique to make your writing interesting. Yet be careful. If you repeat a word or phrase too many times, though you're doing it for emphasis, it can sound dull. To avoid this, change the form as Ralph Waldo Emerson did in this paragraph.

Every day, the sun; and after sunset, Night and her stars. *Ever* the winds blow; *ever* the grass grows. *Every day*, men and women, conversing—beholding and beholden.

From "The American Scholar," *The Complete Writings and Other Writings*, edited by Brooks Atkinson (New York, The Modern Library).

He might have written:

Every day, the sun; and after sunset, Night and her stars. *Every day* the winds blow; *every day* the grass grows. *Every day*, men and women, conversing—beholding and beholden.

Every day would sound monotonous, wouldn't it?

Sometimes you can repeat a word or phrase at the end of one paragraph to pass smoothly into the next, as we'll learn in Chapter 18. For now, here are two examples. In my story about the Nepali hospital, look at the word *blessings*.

From somewhere below I could hear singing. Though the words were Nepalese, I recognized an old hymn, "There Shall Be Showers of Blessings."

"Blessings!" I muttered. "In this place?"

In another example I repeated a question to connect two paragraphs.

I reached up to the top shelf of the cupboard to get a vase for the roses. As my fingers touched it, the vase slipped. It teetered for a second on the edge and crashed to the floor.

My mother came running. She yelled, "What have you done?"

What had I done? Tears splashed down my cheeks for I knew I had broken the vase that had once belonged to my great-great grandmother.

Ad writers know the value of repetition, too. Notice how often they use it in magazines and on television.

The *no-fire, sure-fire* barbecued chicken

Low, low, low prices

It takes a *puppy* a full year to outgrow *Puppy* Chow

As you write your next story, experiment with repetition. Read your piece aloud and circle each word or phrase you've used several times. Look at them carefully. Did you know you were repeating them? Do they add emphasis and interest? If not, cross out those you don't need.

Control your repetition. Use it for a purpose, and you'll see our heads nod not with boredom but with interest. Yes, with interest.

13
Setting the Stage

Now that you know how to keep us awake, you're anxious to get on with your memoirs. Yet you're wondering if you should take time to describe the place where it all happened. Before you decide, think for a minute about the way you feel when you go to the theater. You wait impatiently for the curtain to open. But, when it does, the stage may be empty, as in some modern plays. Two characters enter, but where are they? Outdoors? You see no trees, no houses, no roads. Inside? There's no bed, no table, not even a sofa or chair to sit on. You're confused and disappointed, aren't you?

Your readers are disappointed, too, if you bring your brother or cousin or aunt into your memoirs and leave any of them standing in empty space. Set the stage and let us see where they are and what it's like. Don't just give us the facts, though, like a newspaper reporter. Remember to show, not tell, as you learned to do in Chapter 8.

To show us your scene, you need, first of all, to see it clearly. What time of day or year is it? What is the weather like?

The shock of crisp icicle fingers on my wrist jerked me awake. Dawn crept through the window as the little nurse smiled a good morning.

Watching my breath puff out in the cold, I stared at the thin finger of sunlight pushing through the tall windows.

You know that it is early morning in winter. And it's not snowing or raining because you see that "thin finger of sunlight." But where is this place?

Rewritten, the paragraph tells us.

The shock of crisp icicle fingers on my wrist jerked me awake. Dawn crept through the window as the little Nepali nurse smiled a good morning.

Watching my breath puff out in the cold, I stared at the bleak hospital room with the thick green walls. A thin finger of sunlight pushed through the tall windows. But even that couldn't brighten the lofty ceiling and marble floors of this building that had once been a palace.

"A Blanket of Love," by Fanny-Maude Evans, *Lutheran Women*, April, 1978

Now the stage is set. We know it is a Nepali hospital that had once been a palace. We can see those tall windows, high ceilings and marble floors. Sounds intriguing, doesn't it? We're anxious to find out what happens. Be sure, though, when showing your scene, to include all the important props that affect your story. What kind of bed, mirror, pictures were in that bedroom? How did the desks in the schoolroom and the blackboard and old stove look?

In my memoir of the Japanese inn, our bedroom furnishings seem sparse by Western standards. Yet their simplicity helps to emphasize the peace and beauty of the inn.

I looked around the room as the girls dragged our bag past a low lacquer table. The only piece of furniture, it stood directly in the center between blue zabuton cushions. Beyond it, a tiny alcove held two yellow chrysanthemums in a blue vase beside a slender tree trunk. Peeled and polished, it extended to the ceiling. A painted waterfall on a pine-dotted mountain splashed across a long scroll on the wall behind.

So far, you've been thinking of indoor settings. Now let's look at the outdoor scene. Sky, trees, water, roads, fences, utility poles, buildings. Can you see them? Let's examine the outside of the ryokan.

The little Toyota skittered over cobblestones, stopping in front of a sprawling wood and stucco building.

I stepped down onto a concrete slab that seemed almost to be a part of the street. It extended into the hotel entry between gnarled pines and giant aralias.

You see that the street is cobblestone, the building sprawling and made of wood and stucco. A concrete walk leads to the entry. You see, too, those gnarled pines and giant aralias as you follow along that walk.

Remember to show us exactly what is on your stage. Look at this car, packed for a honeymoon trip.

Herbert's car, a black model-A-Ford convertible, was all packed. It held a tent, sleeping bags, fishing equipment, camp stove, lantern, cooking utensils and food for the two-week camping trip that would take us as far north as Crater Lake in Oregon.

> "My First Wedding Day" by Elfriede Tavernier,
> *Silhouettes of the Past*

If she had written, "His car was all packed for a two-week camping trip," her stage would have been almost empty. But she lets us see this overloaded Ford and each different piece of camping gear.

No matter how many props you place on your memoir stage, your readers will be disappointed unless you show how your characters use them. Remember those lively, active verbs you've already studied? Use them to show the action. Notice the verbs in this paragraph.

The captain crouched in the bow of the boat. He didn't see the wave that reared above him until too late. It reached out, coiled like the arm of a giant octopus around him and jerked him back. He teetered for a second, then shot down into the boiling water.

Crouched, reared, reached, coiled, jerked, teetered, and *shot* all give you a clear picture.

When you watch a play, you see, hear, and sometimes smell. In your story setting, you can also touch and taste. In the piece about the Japanese ryokan you listen not only to sounds but also to silence.

We followed down the silent hall, lighted by the faint glow filtering through the shoji screens. We could hear only the trickle of the stream and the pad of the maid's feet. We met no one. And we didn't speak as we walked softly into this oasis of peace and quiet and solitude.

We all like to touch things, too. A shiny mahogany desk, thick green moss, a soft baby's cheek. Or even a pad on the floor of a Japanese inn.

That night, back in our room, we found that our maid had transformed it. The table had disappeared. Two thick foam rubber pads lay side by side in its place. A plump comforter, as light and warm as down, covered snowy sheets. . . .

The foam pads felt exactly right. But I did inflate my own plastic pillow. The one they'd given me felt like it was stuffed with straw and crackled when I poked it.

In your memoir, the sense of taste, too, can help us see your setting as it does in the South Seas story.

A monstrous wave smashed against the boat. Rick bit down hard on his lip. The taste of blood mingled with salt as the wave roared over him.

You share "the taste of blood mingled with salt" as that monstrous wave hits.

Many of you remember the taste of fresh-baked cinnamon rolls, or ice water on a summer afternoon, or castor oil. Put them in your memoir setting so we can taste them, too.

Don't forget your sense of smell, either. Offensive as well as pleasant odors sharpen your scene. Like this one:

Grandfather was a taxidermist. In two large rooms, huge display cabinets housed his collection of stuffed animals and birds. . . . In one corner he kept his paints and varnishes, a large collection of glass eyes of every imaginable size and color and all the other paraphernalia he needed for his work. There he also killed any live creature brought to him for stuffing. Quite often when he was swamped with work, the dead corpse would be lying around for days, producing a foul odor that was the bane of Grandma's life. . . .

"How often do I have to tell you to keep that darned door shut?" she would say.

> "My Most Prized Possession" by Eugene J. Tavernier,
> *Silhouettes of the Past*

I don't blame Grandma, do you? You want to hold your nose at the thought of this room with its odor of dead animals.

And do use color in your memoir setting. Any stage looks dull in black and white. Show the colors of your props. Look again at the South Seas story.

"That foot's so swelled up it looks like a puffer fish," the captain growled.

He shook his head. "Looks bad."

He ran his fingers over the streaks of greenish purple fanning up from the deep red coral cuts along Rick's ankle.

Can't you see the greenish purple streaks and the deep red cuts? The writer could have left out the color and just told you the foot was swollen. Yet how much clearer it is when you know it was red and greenish purple.

One warning, though, about your memoir setting. At the theater you don't see all of the props at once unless it's a one-act play. So it is with your writing. Don't crowd your stage with each plant you can see from a window, all the cans, packages or boxes on the shelves of the country store, or every dress and hat in the Easter parade. After you show where, what and when, weave the rest of your background through your story. As your characters move from one scene to another, change the settings just as stagehands do for each new act.

If you'd like to practice, try rewriting these sentences to show vivid scenes.

Use specific words and detail

1. It was a hot summer day.
2. He wore a coat.
3. The barn was old.

Use action verbs

1. Rain runs down the roof.
2. All the passengers got off the bus.
3. The bird was injured.

Add color

1. Spring flowers in the garden
2. A storm on a lake
3. Bare branches in a winter sunset

14

A Real Live Character

The stage is set and the actors are waiting in the wings. Will they walk, skip, jump, or stride into your scene? Laughing, yelling, crying? Or do they move like robots and stiff manikins? How can you bring them alive?

First of all, be sure your reader knows who is doing the acting. Are you, the writer? Or are you merely an observer showing us your mother, grandfather, or neighbor?

Generally, you are the star. For, after all, memoirs are your memories. And you will usually use the first person *I* in sharing them.

I hated the white frame house, its paint peeling like sawdust curls from the ancient boards.

Sometimes using the first person is difficult. Most of us tend to feel uncomfortable with so many I's. But when you pick up a magazine and read. "I Was Kidnaped!," it sounds much more intriguing than "Lenore King Was Kidnaped!" The *I* gives you the feeling you are hearing a real story from a real person.

Occasionally, though, a memory may be so painful or personal you don't want to share it in the first person. You may prefer to step back and look at yourself as if you were looking at a self-portrait and write your experience in the third person.

The young teacher's wife hated the white frame house, its paint peeling like sawdust curls from the ancient boards.

You'll use the third person, too, when you tell someone else's story. Now you're an onlooker rather than an actor, and we hear your grandmother, cousin, or friend talking.

My grandmother hated the white frame house, its paint peeling like sawdust curls from the ancient boards.

You can tell this type of story as an outsider without adding any of your feelings or thoughts, or you can make your own observations and comments. Either way, you are still an observer.

I often heard my grandmother say how much she hated the white frame house, its paint peeling like sawdust curls from the ancient boards.

or

I knew how my grandmother felt about the white frame house, its paint peeling like sawdust curls from the ancient boards. She hated it. And I didn't blame her.

Whether it's your story or that of another, let us know all of the people who take part in it. What do you see when you first meet someone? What gives you your first impression? It's the outward appearance. Clothes don't really make a man or woman but they do say something about the person. You can introduce your characters simply by telling us directly what they are wearing.

He wore paint-stained pants and a torn undershirt that might once have been white.
Her faded sweater sagged above a skirt that had lost its pleats, the uneven hem flapping around skinny legs in long black stockings.

She wore a soft pink dress that whispered "Paris."

You can show us a person's clothing indirectly, too, challenging us to use our imaginations.

Her dress fit like it had been molded before it was sewed.
They looked clean but rumpled, as if they'd left their clothes too long in the dryer.
She wore a blouse she must have picked up at a "No Try-ons Sale."

Often the appearance of a person's clothing goes with a job or profession.

The mechanic wiped his hands on grease-stained overalls.
A woman in nurse's white hurried up the steps.
He wore the badge of a teacher, perennial chalk dust on his sleeve.

Maybe clothes don't impress you when you meet someone but a face or a figure does. Often only one or two details can show us physical appearance.

It may be a face. Is it round, oval, pale, acne-scarred, sallow?

The slim oval face of a girl just emerging from childhood
A face eroded by decades of hardship
A profile clean and hard, chipped only a little by the years
A sad face full of shadows

Perhaps it's the eyes that you notice especially. They can tell you a great deal about someone. Mean, velvety, narrow, round, clear, intense eyes all carry messages about their owners.

Gray eyes smoldering under a scowl
Marble eyes in a granite face

Clear, intense blue eyes
Round, innocent eyes
Eyes screened by thick gold-rimmed glasses

A person's mouth may give us a hint about a character.
What kind of smile does he or she have? Teeth? Lips?

A commercial smile, pasted on
Laugh rings rippling out from the pool of his smile
A clean, toothpaste smile
Licking her lips to wet a nervous smile
Lips pulled back from tight, irregular teeth
Upper teeth protruding as though perennially ready to bite
The rigid set of his mouth

Hair says something about a person, too. A friend who
works in a beauty shop always notices hair first when she
meets someone. She insists the hair style a person chooses
tells a lot about character. What kind of man still insists on
a crew cut? Or a shaved head? Or has the latest mod
styling complete with permanent? What sort of woman
swishes long waist-length hair as she passes? Wears it
pulled back in a bun? Or has a short pixie cut?

A straight line of bangs accenting a face
A cowlick no amount of brushing could defeat
Spiky hair sticking up in back
Snow-white hair rippling up from her temples

And what about hands? Do they hint at character? Artists think so. Remember the famous painting "Praying
Hands"? It has been molded into bookends, cast in
bronze, and printed on calendars as well as immortalized
in oils. Of course you can't sculpture or paint your characters' hands. But you can show us a word picture. Are they

rough, damp, callused, or neatly manicured? And how are they used? Does your cousin or friend clench fists, crack knuckles, or let open palms lie loose in a lap?

Long, slim fingers tipped with coral

A big, heavy palm falling like a rock on his knee

Nibbling at the ragged tip of a frustrated fingernail

Quiet hands at rest in her lap

Fingernails permanently edged with grease

And how do the people you are showing us stand and walk? Do they slump, stretch up tall, hunch over? Do they shuffle, skip, totter, tiptoe, or limp into your story?

She stood tall and straight like a princess, though she'd lost her kingdom.

Taller than her husband, she habitually hunches as though to meet him eye to eye.

Barely five and a half feet tall, he strutted like a banty rooster, always ready to fight.

My mother in her eightieth year still walked with a spring that said she was going somewhere.

My neighbor bustled about the kitchen like a round, plump hen.

Big and bony and gray, he lumbered toward her.

He stumbled toward the stairs, listing slightly to windward.

Remember, you don't need to show all of these physical characteristics. Only one or two will let us meet your character. But do your readers really know this person? So far, we have only an outward impression. We need to share emotions to really get acquainted. We may not like them, but whether we like them or not, we need to feel them. You can use direct description and simply tell us how your mother or brother or friend felt.

He felt the cold slither of fear along his spine.

She was so happy she wanted to dance.

As metal ground against metal he felt sick, the sickness of remembering his insurance had lapsed.

She was tired, so tired—would sleep never come?

Tell us how a character feels if it's someone appearing only briefly in your memoirs. But share much more intensely the feelings of a character we'll meet more often. Let us really feel anger, heartbreak, pity, love, excitement, through action.

He shifted his glasses on his nose, faster and faster, in increasing irritation.

She was so excited she forgot to put her lipstick on.

Anger tightened his jaw into ugly knots.

She ran her fingertips over her eyes, pushing away the tears.

Let us know something about your characters' traits, too. The list of traits is almost endless: ambition, jealousy, honesty, pride, patience, shyness, boldness, laziness.

He took off the only coat he owned and wrapped it around the shivering young soldier.

The trait he showed is compassion or generosity.

She worked hard to keep from working.

This trait, of course, is laziness.

One dominant trait lets us see what your character is like. But nobody is all good or all bad. Sometimes a person has a secondary trait that seems contradictory. For example, a character can be gentle but stubborn, honest but impulsive, generous but cautious, short-tempered but soft-hearted, stern but loving.

He donated $1,000 to the refugee fund but insisted his wife do the laundry by hand when the washer broke down.

This man seems generous but inconsiderate.

She speaks with authority but ignores challenging questions.

This person shows confidence in her own knowledge but shows resentment or even fear when it is challenged.

Quite often you can give a brief picture of a character in one sentence. Think of these questions:

Why is this person unique?
What sets the character apart to make you remember him or her?

He had the fresh look of a man who loved the out-of-doors.

She hid her insecurity behind thick layers of makeup.

He was still a country boy beneath his city veneer.

David McCullough, accepting a National Book Award for *The Path Between the Seas: The Creation of the Panama Canal* (Simon and Schuster), said, "History is people and if the research and writing of history is sometimes difficult, it is because people are difficult to know. But without the feel of life all that we struggle to say about the past, to record and save and pass on, all the names and dates and shelves of data are of little consequence."

Now, let's practice putting the feel of life into your characters.

1. Write a brief sketch, showing, by outward description only, a person you know or remember. You don't need to show

everything a character is wearing or all the details of appearance.

2. Rewrite your character sketch, letting us share emotions and actions.

3. Show us the same character in one sentence.

15

Did They Really Say That?

Now your readers know how your characters look, dress, and feel. But something's missing. How do they sound?

One of the best ways of all to characterize is by conversation. Dialogue is like playing catch. One person tosses the ball, another catches and returns it. One person speaks, then another. Back and forth. Their words help bring them to life.

If someone answers the phone, "Hello. Whatcha want?" it could be a child. But "Good morning. William Jones speaking. May I help you?" might be your banker.

We all have more than one vocabulary, too. Words we read or write tend to be formal. We would never use some of them in speaking.

WRITTEN: During the Depression there was a considerable decline in consumer buying.

SPOKEN: During the Depression nobody had much money to spend.

People talking interrupt each other. They leave some sentences unfinished, speak in fragments.

"George has been transferred."
"Where?"
"New York, and—"
"But I thought—"
"Well, you thought wrong."

Most of us use slang, but be careful of it in your writing. Words like *heck, gee whiz, gosh, kiddo* are definitely dated. Audrey B. Eaglen, writing in *School Library Journal,* says, "If you must use slang, be prepared to listen to it first-hand and constantly, since it changes almost daily." If your father or uncle dotted his conversation with *shucks, drat,* or *darn,* do the same when you're quoting him. But be sure any slang you write is appropriate to the period when your characters lived. Don't let them say *cool* or *tough* or *all right, man* in the early 1900s.

Be sure, though, that you do use their distinctive vocabularies. All of us have our own way with words. We acquire certain idioms and phrases from the region where we grew up and from our training, education, and experience.

In Boston, you *bear left* or *bear right,* not *turn left* or *turn right.* In Kentucky, if a friend offers to carry you home, he does not mean to pick you up bodily. He's just offering you a ride. And if he asks for a poke, don't hit him. He wants a paper bag. In Colorado, people look at you strangely if you say rode'o with the accent on the *de.* They pronounce the word ro'deo, accenting *ro.*

And we use different words when speaking to different people. In church, greeting a minister, we might say, "Good morning, Dr. Wilson. It's a beautiful day, isn't it?" But, turning to a friend, we'd say, "Hi, Anne. Isn't this an absolutely super morning?"

Remember, too, when you write dialogue for your characters, that we need to meet them before we hear them. Let us know how they look and feel *before* they speak.

Ed shifted his big frame, his hands clenching and unclenching. "Mister, those are fighting words where I come from," he said.

Bright dots of anger flamed in her cheeks. "What are you saying?" she asked. "That I neglect my baby?"

Let us hear a voice, too. How does it sound? Can you relate it to something familiar?

His voice sounded angry. "You get outta here!" he said. "And don't never come back."

By his words you know he is angry. But can you really hear him? Listen again.

His voice had a rumble like a roll of thunder. "You get outta here!" he roared. "And don't never come back!"

Now you can hear his anger, rumbling like thunder.

"Bobby's gone. We can't find him." Her voice was shrill.

That sentence doesn't give much of an idea, really, about her voice, does it? But revise it, comparing it to a shrill sound.

"Bobby's gone. We can't find him." Her voice rose like the sound of an approaching siren.

Can't you hear that voice rising?

Your character's speech patterns are important, too. Does the uncle you are writing about speak in short, clipped sentences? Does he ramble, talk fast, mumble, stutter?

"I am extremely disappointed in you and I cannot understand why any young man would wish to become a school dropout. Please explain your actions," my uncle said in his stern school-teacher voice.

"I hate s-s-school. I hate b-b-books. I hate t-t-teachers," my brother stuttered.

Besides giving us a picture of the person who is speaking, you can use dialogue to show us a character through the eyes of someone else. Two people talking or gossiping can give us a picture of a third.

"How long do you think Nancy'll stay with Bill?" Helen asked. "About six months?"

"Well, maybe seven." Her sister stirred two spoons of sugar into her coffee. "Soon as she finds out she didn't marry a big spender, it's goodbye, Bill. She always did think marriage has dollar signs."

In writing dialogue, you need to watch out for certain words. Adverbs can creep in without you knowing it and weaken your writing. Use them sparingly, if at all. Let their words and the way they speak show how your characters feel.

"Stop!" she said forcefully.
"Don't cry," he said consolingly.
"Why are we going?" he asked questioningly.

Do you really need *forcefully, consolingly, questioningly?* "Stop!" is forceful. "Don't cry" tells us he is consoling, and we know "Why are we going?" is a question. Go over your writing and underline all of your adverbs. See if you can leave them out.

Said is another word you can often do without. It's a perfectly good word, and many famous writers use it constantly to let us know who is talking. But, for variety, try such words as *interrupted, replied, added, emphasized.* And, if only two people are speaking, you may find you can eliminate *said* altogether after you identify them.

Jim slammed the kitchen door. "Hi, Mom," he said.
She looked up from scrubbing the floor. "Hi, Jimmy. How'd everything go?"
"O.K., I guess."

"Only O.K? What happened to *fine?*"
"Well, sure wasn't nothin' fine about this day."

After the first two speak, you've told us who's talking. If their conversation is long, though, we may forget. Be sure to remind us, after a paragraph or two. Of course you won't let your characters ramble on and on or we'll lose interest. Break up Aunt Minnie's monologue or Grandpa George's story with some kind of action. Let the wind blow, a door slam, a dog bark. Someone may come in, pull out a chair, stand up or go out.

"I don't think I'll go to that wedding," I said to my husband. "Ever since that kid was born I've counted on having her get married right here in our own church. With showers and parties and all our friends. It's downright embarrassing that she won't come home for the biggest event of her life. What in the world will we tell everybody? I sure don't know. Maybe I should write her. Tell her just what I think of all these plans she's making. Maybe she'll come to her senses."

By now you're tired of this wedding and have lost interest. But break up this long speech and see what happens.

"I don't think I'll go to that wedding," I said.
My husband looked up from his paper. "Why not?"
"Why not? Why, ever since that kid was born I've counted on having her get married right here in our own church. With showers and parties and all our friends."
He wrinkled his forehead above his glasses.
"It's not your wedding, you know."
"Well, it's downright embarrassing that she won't come home for the biggest event of her life. What in the world will we tell everybody?"
He let the paper drop to the floor. "What's the matter with you? She's the one getting married. You're not."

"I know that!" I snapped. "But I think I'll write and tell her just what I think of all these plans she's making. Maybe she'll come to her senses."

Very likely you want to read on, now, to find out what happens.

Remember, too, when you're writing dialogue, to use a new paragraph each time a different person speaks.

Bob put an arm across his daughter's shoulders. "Don't work so hard, kid. You don't have to finish that sewing tonight, do you?"

"Yes I do, Dad." Connie bit the end off her thread. "I got to finish it for Mom's birthday tomorrow."

"Holy Toledo!" Bob jumped up. "Is that tomorrow? Sure a good thing you reminded me."

Notice that you put action or description that goes along with a speaker's words all in the same paragraph.

"I don't want to go," the child wailed. His nose was red from crying and he kept wiping a grubby hand across his eyes.

Notice, too, that you set off verbs like *said, spoke, answered,* with commas or other appropriate punctuation.

"I guess it's O.K.," she said, "but I still don't like it."
"Come on!" he shouted. "Or we'll never make it."

Place commas, periods, question marks, and exclamation points inside the quotation marks.

"Well, I saw her," Don said, "taking tickets at the show last night."

The teacher tried to keep her voice calm. "Just sit down and be quiet."

"What's going on, Al?" Dave called. "Why are you yelling?"

Mary shouted at the toddler, "Get away from that water! Right now!"

If a speech is more than one paragraph long, place quotation marks at the beginning of each new paragraph but only at the end of the final paragraph.

"It's always a surprise to me who my kids choose to marry," my neighbor said. "But even though I don't like their choice, I go along with it. Of course I have doubts. What parent doesn't? But if you've taught your kids to make their own decisions you have to respect them now.

"Another thing." She took a deep breath. "If your in-law doesn't like his own parents he may just transfer all his complaints to you. One of my daughters-in-law did just that. She had a bossy mother and every time I opened my mouth she'd bristle up. I sure had to be careful for a while.

"And whatever you do," she went on, "don't rush up and kiss your new in-law child. He just may not be used to it."

What about thoughts? Do we enclose them in quotation marks? It all depends. Do enclose thoughts that sound as if the person is speaking to someone else in quotation marks. These thoughts are written in first person.

The phone jangled on the wall just outside Mary's room. She sat up in bed, rubbing her eyes. "Why, oh why does my dad have to be a doctor?" she thought as she heard his voice in the hall. "Always running off to some emergency in the middle of the night. Waking us all up. Why can't he be just a farmer or a teacher so we can get some sleep?"

Thoughts that you, the writer, tell us are not enclosed in quotation marks. And they are in the third person.

The phone jangled on the wall just outside Mary's room. She sat up in bed, rubbing her eyes. Why, oh why did her dad have to be a doctor, she thought, as she heard his voice in the hall. Always running off to some emergency in the night. Waking them all up. Why couldn't he just be a farmer or a teacher so they could get some sleep?

If you add your own interpretation of Mary's thoughts, you do not enclose these in quotation marks either. They, too, are in the third person.

The phone jangled on the wall just outside Mary's room. She sat up in bed, rubbing her eyes. Irritation surged through her mind as she wondered why her dad had to be a doctor. She hated all the emergencies that woke them up in the night. She wished, somehow, she could wave a magic wand and change him into an ordinary farmer or a teacher so they all could get some sleep.

Ready to practice? Write a conversation between two people you remember well. Let us hear their tone, their vocabulary, the sound of their words. You might choose some of the following:

1. Your father speaking to your brother who has just brought the car home with a crumpled fender
2. You and your sister disagreeing about who should dry the dishes
3. You and your grandfather discussing your plans to stay out all night on graduation night
4. An aunt and uncle arguing about the best methods to use in planting the garden
5. Or a conversation between any other two people you remember

16

Spice Up Your Story—Use an Anecdote

You've worked for hours on your memoir. You've filled your wastebasket with crumpled paper and emptied it twice. And still your story has the blahs. What can you do? You might use an anecdote.

Yet, what exactly is an anecdote? I like writer Harry Edward Neal's definition: "A brief story involving people in action." And I might add that the brief story is a single incident.

Anecdotes have been with us, I'm sure, since prehistoric times, when a caveman came home and told of his narrow escape from an angry mammoth. Aesop, that ancient Greek writer of animal fables, was a master at creating anecdotes. And we find many of these small stories, like the parable of the Good Samaritan, in the Bible. But what really is their purpose?

Just as this chapter title says, they spice up your story. Remember you can use an anecdote to hook your reader in your beginning as I did in my story about color-blindness.

During the Depression, when I met Paul, I had no idea he couldn't tell a ripe strawberry from a green one.

"Say, I like that dress," he said one night when we were waiting in line for a movie. "That shade of pink is especially nice."

"Who're you kidding?" I burst out. "I never wear pink. This dress is mint green."

"But—" He stopped. "Oh, sure. I should have known. Might as well tell you. I'm color-blind."

"A Different Kind of Rainbow" by Fanny-Maude Evans,
Elks Magazine, November, 1972

Right away you probably want to know more about this color-blind man.

You can end your piece with an anecdote, too, as Sue Scofield did in her story about a desert postmistress. Though the woman lived in a town so arid that water was almost as scarce as green grass, she planted a tree in front of her shack. Through the years she watered it with bath, dish, and wash water.

When she retired, she shook the dust of the desert from her long skirts, moved to Santa Monica and again put on the styles of the day.

How did she get rid of her old shack? When I asked, she said an old miner came along, paid her cash and sat himself down under the tree. She asked him, "Don't you want to see the house?"

He replied, "Nope, I bought the tree."

"Desert Postmistress" by Sue Scofield,
Silhouettes of the Past

An anecdote can emphasize a point, too. We all understand and remember a story much better than an ordinary statement. See how one writer did this in a story about her brother who liked to knit.

Though Dave enjoys his hobby, he is not a liberated man. He doesn't tell many people about it. For they seem to react strangely. Especially women. Once, when he went into a store to buy yarn, the clerk asked, "Are you sure these are the colors your wife wants?"

Dave drew himself up to his full six feet. "They're not for my wife," he growled. "I'm the one knitting the sweater."

The girl stared at him for a minute. Then she leaned over the counter and whispered, "You don't want anybody to know, do you?"

The writer could have written:

When Dave went into the store to buy some yarn, the clerk assumed he didn't want anybody to know that he knitted.

But it wouldn't have made the point nearly as well.

Anecdotes can help, too, in setting your stage, as this one does.

Bernie Kingery, long time avalanche expert, sat in his office in the stout A-frame building at Alpine Meadows in the Sierras. Anxiously he operated the radio transmitter, checking on the freak spring blizzard that had suspended visitor skiing. When he heard the outside door creak he looked up. Two young staff members, Frank Yateman and Anna Conrad, were stomping snow from their boots.

Bernie scowled. "You shouldn't have come out in this storm. Avalanche danger is serious."

"We're worried about our car buried in the snow," Frank said.

Bernie softened. "Better stay here. This building's built to withstand heavy snowfall."

Minutes later they heard an ominous rumbling and swishing. The avalanche moved at express train speed. The powerful blast of displaced air it pushed before it slammed into the building like an explosion. Tons of snow thundered down after it. Stout beams buckled and cracked. . . . Snow pushed inexorably into every space, twenty or thirty feet deep.

Now all was quiet—too quiet. The building had become a giant snowpile.

Helen Rogers Creighton

You can see this avalanche roaring down the mountain, can't you? And don't you want to know what happened to Bernie and Frank and Anna?

A small story adds life and stimulates interest, even to a subject you might not ordinarily find appealing. Like iguanas.

During WWII, I served as a nurse in Panama. One morning as I headed for my quarters, I heard a noise in a palm tree near me, as though one of the fronds was being rippled. I glanced up in time to see something green hurtle toward me and plump into the grass at my feet. For a moment I felt the fear and panic born of being faced with the unknown. I moved back.

A shiny green reptile about two feet long with perhaps half of its length devoted to tail lay unmoving in the grass. With four legs and a skin that resembled that of a snake, the creature had the appearance of one of the monsters pictured in the books on prehistoric animal life. Its black beadlike eyes stared at me. A film of skin covered them for a moment. It blinked again, then scurried around the base of the palm and into the heavy grass, completely camouflaged.

This was my introduction to the iguana.

"The Indelicate Delicacy" by Doris Bona,
Silhouettes of the Past

Sometimes, with an anecdote, you can say a lot in a small space.

On a cold winter morning in 1909, Charles D. Herrold climbed to the roof of his house in San Jose, California, and put up a radio aerial.

"Are you crazy?" a neighbor yelled from the sidewalk below. "What are you doing?"

"Putting up an aerial," Dr. Herrold answered. "One day your house and everybody else's will have a pole on top."

See how these few sentences introduce us to Dr. Herrold and the dream he had that some day everyone would listen to a radio? Use an anecdote this way to condense your story.

Often you can show us more about a character with an anecdote than any other way.

In the late 1800's my grandparents settled on a Texas homestead. Shortly after her first son was born, my grandmother discovered she was pregnant again. She said to my grandfather, "Henry, I'll give you a choice. I'll either cook or have babies, but I won't do both."

She never cooked.

Already you know that Grandmother is a strong-minded woman.

You can see, now, why it's important to use anecdotes in your writing. But how do you go about it?

Though it's the shortest short story of all, the anecdote should have the same qualities as a longer tale. It should interest and entertain us and be something we can identify with. It should have action, characters, complications, and a satisfactory ending or twist. Whether you remember the incidents in your anecdotes exactly as they happened or not, they must sound true. Give names of people, dates or time, and location. Notice how this student put them in her introductory anecdote about cutting silhouettes.

It was a rainy Iowa day in August of 1932. The children were all busy with old magazines and scissors, cutting out pictures to paste into scrapbooks for safekeeping.

Five-year-old Dick was on the floor with a big piece of paper and his crayons. He was trying to make a man. . . . Dick didn't seem pleased with the man he was drawing, so he came to me with his paper and crayon. As he put them on the table he said, "Mom, make me a man." I picked up a piece of paper and reached for a pair of scissors.

"Now, Dick," I said, "look that way." I turned his head so I could see his profile and started cutting the shape of his neck and under his chin. Then I did his lower lip, his upper lip and his little round nose. Next, I cut his forehead, over his head and down the back. It was done. I looked at it carefully and it was like him. I had cut a silhouette. It was the first silhouette I had ever seen cut.

"A Talent for Cutting" by Avis Kurtzweil,
Silhouettes of the Past

In writing your anecdote, show us the action. Use vivid words, specific details, and color. Look again at this memoir of our travels in Europe, where we were constantly getting lost.

In Spain, we were lost once more after taking a detour on a narrow dirt road. Pulling over beside an orange grove, we unfolded our map.

A young man with a farmer's tan vaulted over the fence to lean on our car window. We traced the dark line of the highway and in primitive Spanish asked how to find it. The man scowled at the map. He ran back to the orchard, grabbed up a sack of oranges and tossed it into our car. Was our Spanish that bad? Had we mixed up highways and oranges?

But the farmer pushed a motorbike out from behind a shed, jumped on and roared down the road, waving to us to follow. Kilometer after kilometer we twisted and turned around hairpin curves until at last we came to the highway.

With a smart salute the young Spaniard sped away.

"The Magic Map" by Fanny-Maude Evans,
Odyssey, March-April, 1981

If your characters are talking, let them tell the story. See how the conversation makes the entire point in this anecdote.

Shopping at the supermarket with her three-year-old son, Danny, my sister spent half her time wrestling bubble gum packs, boxes of sugar cereal and bags of licorice from the little boy. As she replaced each on the shelf, Danny's cries mounted to screams. At the meat counter, his shrieks drowned out his mother's order.

The butcher leaned over the counter. "Hey, kid!" he said, his face stern. "See that sign?" He pointed to a cardboard square on the wall proclaiming, "Fresh Fryers—69¢ a lb."

The toddler looked up, still sobbing.

"Know what it says?" the butcher asked.

Danny shook his head. "Uh-uh."

"No crying allowed," the big man read. "Understand?"

The child's eyes widened. He stared up at the sign, gulped and swallowed a final sob.

Use an anecdote not only to make a point clear, but to get to it quickly. In this story the writer introduces the idea right away with an anecdote.

Kathy stormed across the street and into my kitchen. Clutching her six-week-old son like a shield on her arm, she snapped, "I've had it with Tom! I can't stand that guy another minute."

She rubbed at her puffy eyes. "Know what he did this morning? Had the nerve to get mad because a button was off his shirt. How can I think of buttons with diapers and formulas and everything?"

Poor Kathy, I thought, pouring her a cup of coffee. She needs a love account.

"Try a Love Account," by Fanny-Maude Evans,
Lady's Circle, September, 1975

And do be sure to end your anecdote with a surprise or punch to give it snap. In this piece about a trip into the interior of Brazil the writer surprises us in the ending.

On the dirt pathway, everyone watched us. Men greeted us with low whistles and suggestive smirks.

"I don't like this," Evelyn said. "What's it all about?"

"I'm not sure," I said. "But I'm afraid I can guess." I looked down at our jeans. "We're a long way from the big city, you know. And I forgot that back here in the jungle, pants mean just one thing. They're the badge of a street woman."

Now try writing an anecdote or two just for practice. Then take another look at that story that gave you so much trouble. Add some anecdotes. Maybe you can begin or end with one or get into the story faster. Work on it and you'll soon find that your memoir is full of spice instead of the blahs.

17

Creeping Clutter

In writing your memoirs you've been learning to paint pictures with words. In these word pictures, as in paintings, it's important to know what to leave out.

Today, clutter creeps like a disease into our language. It spouts from our newspapers and TVs. It confuses school and business memos and thrives in government tracts and political orations. Thomas Jefferson once said, "The most valuable of all talents is that of never using two words when one will do." His friend Benjamin Franklin agreed in this story.

When I was a journeyman printer, one of my companions, an apprentice Hatter, having served out his time, was about to open a shop for himself. His first concern was to have a hand-some signboard, with a proper inscription. He composed it in these words: "John Thompson, Hatter, makes and sells hats for ready money," with a figure of a hat subjoined. But he thought he would submit it to his friends for their amendments. The first he shewed it to thought the word "hatter" tautologous, because followed by the words "makes hats" which shew he was a hat-ter. It was struck out. The next observed that the word "makes" might as well be omitted, because his customers would not care who made the hats. If good and to their mind, they would buy, by whomsoever made. He struck it out. A third said he thought the words "for ready money" were useless as it was not the custom of the place to sell on credit. Everyone who purchased expected to pay. They were parted with, and the inscription now stood "John Thompson sells hats." "Sells" says his next friend? "Why nobody will expect you to give them away. What then is the use of that word?" It was stricken out and "hats" followed it, the rather, as there was one painted on the board. So his inscription was reduced ultimately to "John Thompson" with the figure of a hat subjoined.

Benjamin Franklin. Quoted in a letter written by
Thomas Jefferson to Robert Walsh, December 4, 1818

You can trim your writing just as the hatter did. All those unnecessary words get in our way and slow us down when we read your stories. Begin by looking for needless repetition, words that mean the same thing. One writer calls them "baby puppies," because a puppy is a baby and you don't need that word with it. You might call them dropout words because when you drop them out nobody misses them. Check this list of words you can drop. See how many you use in your writing. No doubt you can add others. Drop the words in parentheses.

(absolutely) sure	(equally) as well
(absolutely) complete	(exactly) identical
(advance) planning	(female) cow
(brief) moment	(first) began
bind (together)	flee (away)
(clearly) apparent	for (the purpose of)
close (proximity)	future (prospects)
continue (on)	(genuine) sincerity
(current) news	I (personally)
(dead) corpse	(in order) to
each (and every one)	(immediately) adjoining
each (and every)	joined (together)
(entirely) complete	(joint) cooperation

(local) neighbors
(located) at
mean it (sincerely)
(more) certain
(more) perfect
(most) unique
(natural) instinct
(necessary) requirements
(new) innovation
(now) pending
(old) adage
(original) creation
(past) history
(personal) history
(personal) friend

(personal) feeling
(personal) opinion
(personal) physician
plan (ahead)
(present) incumbent
raining (outside)
refer (back)
repeat (again)
(same) identical
share (together)
(short) minute
(still) persists
(sum) total
(true) facts
(verbal) discussion

And do you suffer from what writer Andrew Offut calls verycoholism? *Very punctual, very latest, very personal, very good* or *very bad,* even *very pregnant* clutter our writing. Offut found sixty-eight words he could substitute for *very*. Often you can just leave *very* out. Or be specific. Tell us exactly what you mean. You might write:

Tom is very punctual.

How punctual? Exactly on time? Half an hour early? Revise it like this:

Tom is so punctual he always has to wait ten or fifteen minutes for everyone.

Watch out for up-smanship, too. *Face up, head up, rise up, fill up, lift up, polish up, free up* are only a few of the *up* words. These verbs don't need help from the preposition *up*. Leave it out.

Take a hard look, too, at *who, which, that, it* and *there*.

Of course, many times they are necessary. Yet be sure you really need them.

You might write:

The man who was driving the car was my brother.

Try again without the *who*.

The man driving the car was my brother.
                          or
The driver of the car was my brother.

Now try *which*.

The house, which was painted yellow, was easy to sell.

Cross out the *which* and *was*.

The house, painted yellow, was easy to sell.

And do you need *that* in this sentence?

Jim said that he could do nothing about it.

Take out *that*.

Jim said he could do nothing about it.

Do you begin a lot of sentences with *it* and *there?*

It is necessary for him to take that trip.
There are too many boys standing in line.

Look twice at sentences like these. You can probably rewrite them and make them sharper by taking out *it* and *there*.

He must take that trip.
Too many boys are standing in line.

Leave out, too, pretentious words you don't need. Use plain, simple language in your writing. Some of you may remember Franklin Roosevelt's famous line in his first inaugural speech. He said, "We have nothing to fear but fear itself." What if he had said, "At this point in time when fear impacts us, we have the option of facing that impact"? Would any of you have remembered it?

Make all your words count. Speak to your reader in everyday language. It's clearer and easier to understand. Look at this list of words you can simplify. Those in parentheses are perfectly good words, but use them sparingly. I'm sure you can think of many more.

(anticipate) expect
(apparent) clear
(at the present time) now
(at this point in time) now
(commence) begin
(contact) meet
(directive) order, instructions
(essential) necessary
(focus on) discuss
(in position to) can

(initial) first
(implement) do, carry out
(locality) place
(on a few occasions) occasionally
(prior to) before
(proceed) go
(purchase) buy
(remainder) rest
(state) say
(sufficient) enough

Jargon is another form of clutter. In the 1800s it meant nonsensical or unintelligible speech. But today it is the specialized language of scientists, educators, physicians, lawyers, and people in certain trades.

No one objects to special professions and industries using a special vocabulary to exchange information with their colleagues. But, in this day of instant communication, jargon spills over into our common language. Some of it enriches but most of it is so obscure that it only adds clutter. We all know what *input* and *the bottom line* mean. But what is a *motorized attendance module*? Translated, it is a school bus, but only an educator could interpret it. And how about a *wellness resource center*, meaning a hospital, *negative deficit* for *profit*, a *correctional facility* for a *prison?* Why not just use the simple word we all understand?

And then there are fad words like *experiencing, rip-off, laid-back, root cause, up front.* They usually fade out of the language sooner or later. Unfortunately, though, some of the most tiresome, like "Have a good day," stay with us. Originally it was a fresh, pleasant expression. Now, you wince as you hear it from morning until midnight. Eventually it may become as neutral as "How do you do?"

Politicians and industry leaders, as well as others, love another sort of fad word. They attach *wise* to practically any noun. William Strunk, Jr., and E. B. White, in *The Elements of Style*, say, "There is not a noun in the language to which -*wise* cannot be added if the spirit moves one to do so. The sober writer will abstain from the use of this wild syllable."

Newswise, saleswise, colorwise, soulwise, jobwise are just a few of these fad words coined by writers and speakers. Be careful of them in your writing. They soon become clichés.

What is a cliché?

It's a wornout word or expression. When the first person dropped it into the language, it seemed fresh and clever. Listeners picked it up and repeated it. Over and over and over. It echoed and re-echoed so many times that its original meaning was lost. Language expert William Zinsser says, "If a phrase comes to you easily, look at it with deep suspicion. It's probably a cliché." How many times have you heard "food for thought," "on pins and needles," "the picture of health"?

Clichés, like anecdotes, have been around for a long time. The Bible has given us, in one form or another, such expressions as "an eye for an eye," "in the sweat of your brow," "a labor of love." Fresh and new in Biblical times, they were repeated so often they became clichés.

Shakespeare, too, had a talent for novel expressions that became clichés. One student objected to studying his work. "I don't like his plays," she said. "They're too full of clichés." She didn't know that phrases like "more sinned against than sinning," "a pound of flesh," and "to breathe [one's] last" were as fresh as new paint when Shakespeare created them.

A cliché is usually a general statement. "He lived to a ripe old age." What is a ripe old age? Sixty-five? Seventy? Ninety?

Here's another: "They live the good life." One person might find the good life in a palace. Another could prefer a cabin on a mountainside. It's different for each of us.

And look at this one: "All work and no play . . ." What kind of work? What kind of play? Work for some might be play for others and vice versa.

Here again you need to be specific, to use details in your word picture. Show us exactly what you mean.

You'll find clichés in many forms. Some are foreign. *"Et tu, Brute,"* you may remember if you studied Latin. Literally translated "Thou too, Brutus," spoken by Caesar when he saw his friend among his assassins, the phrase came to mean treachery from a friend. *"Tempus fugit,"* another expression from Latin, means "time flies." And some of you may remember that French expression popular during World War I, *"Cherchez la femme."* Translated, it means "look for the woman," implying that a woman was at the bottom of some problem. You don't hear it often today, since the status of women has changed.

Dickens first wrote "dull as ditch water" when he had Fanny Cleaver say, in *Our Mutual Friend*, "He'd be sharper than a serpent's tooth, if he wasn't as dull as ditch water." When I was growing up, I heard it as "dull as dishwater."

And how many of you have written this bit of trivia over and over in your high school yearbook?

> Roses are red, violets are blue,
> Sugar is sweet, and so are you.

Such rhyming verses, which sounded musical and different originally, eventually wear out and become clichés. And so do catchy phrases.

"A pleasure and a privilege" seemed clever in the beginning, as did "a sight for sore eyes," "high and dry," "safe and sound." Old sayings, too, change to empty statements when we hear them too many times. "All good things must come to an end," "Keep a stiff upper lip," and "Penny wise and pound foolish," once snapped you to attention. Today, they sound stuffy, if not boring.

And figures of speech, novel and new the first few times you hear them, soon become clichés. "Burned to a crisp," "dead as a doornail," "old as the hills," now seem dull and mark an outdated writer.

Though many clichés soon wear out, some infiltrate our language and become a part of our speech. "On the rocks," "at loose ends," "blind ambition," "holding your own" are just a few. You cannot speak or write without using clichés every day. But you can try to change them in some way to bring freshness to an old phrase. "Teach an old dog new food tricks," "cold as ice cream," "as hungry as a bear just out of hibernation," and "man does not live by beauty alone" all have a new sound.

Sometimes, too, a cliché is the best way to express an idea. Yet, like dropout words and jargon, clichés can clutter your writing when you use them too often.

Remember, though, when writing dialogue, you need "baby puppies," jargon, and clichés. All of us use them in conversation, some more than others. You might hear anyone say, "I personally can state that there's no skeleton in her closet."

Check the words and phrases that clutter. Strike them out or change them when you can. For practice, see if you can rid these sentences of the kinds of clutter discussed here. Some you need to rewrite.

1. She must repeat the course again.
2. This is the very latest style.
3. It kills bugs dead.
4. He did it on his initial attempt.
5. How will you implement his suggestion?
6. Each and every one must go to school.
7. He's busy as a bee.
8. They were doomed to disappointment.
9. She looks fresh as a daisy.
10. Anne is an actress who is very talented.
11. We crept into the house, which was haunted.
12. Jim didn't like the book that he bought.
13. We expect the joint cooperation of every member.
14. It is apparent that she doesn't like the dress.

18
Engineering Your Memoir Road — Paragraphs

Now that you've cleared away the clutter from your writing, let's see how you're putting it all together.

Remember, writing is like going on a journey, traveling by car from point to point along a highway. On your writing highway you travel by paragraphs to reach your destination.

In man's earliest writing, we find no paragraphs. The Greeks invented them to point to different parts of a manuscript. But they used only a mark in the margin instead of indenting to separate segments.

In writing your paragraph your first sentence is the most important. You probably learned long ago in a composition class that you must have a topic sentence to begin each paragraph. It's still a good idea, for that first sentence tells us what the paragraph is about or what is to come. Let's look at some topic sentences.

When there was time we strolled down the main street to see the gaslights turned on.

From this beginning you expect to find out more about the gaslights in the paragraph.

Our next big moment came ten miles farther down the road.

This first sentence signals that the paragraph will tell you what that next big moment was.

And how long should your paragraphs be? In school, your teacher may have told you never to write a single sentence as a paragraph. Forget that advice. To startle or emphasize, a paragraph can be one sentence or even one word.

An ocean catapult crashed against the boat. It filled almost to the gunwales. The captain's voice boomed out.
"Bail!"
Grabbing cans, the crew shot into action, their faces grim.

Doesn't that one-word paragraph "Bail!" say more than several sentences could? And doesn't that single-sentence paragraph that follows hit you with the shock the crew felt? Such one-word or one-sentence paragraphs move action ahead fast. You race along your writing road. But don't use too many at once. You'll get out of breath and so will we.

And remember how tiresome a road can be, stretching mile after mile in a straight line? You need curves and bridges and tunnels, even detours, to keep from drowsing. So it is with your paragraphs. We soon lose interest in blocks of unbroken print.

Look at your paragraphs. Try to keep most of them short. Yet too many short paragraphs all together can be distracting. Add a longer one, now and then. But be careful. Too many long paragraphs, like too many miles of straight road, can be dull and tiresome. Are yours like this one?

His lips pressed in a thin, tight line, he slammed the door and stamped off to work. Drooping with the weight of my anger, I added the breakfast dishes to the pile in the sink. I ought to clean the kitchen, I thought. I looked with dull eyes at the toast crumbs under the table and the sticky circle of orange juice spilled in front of the refrigerator. Even the calendar hung at a crooked angle. And today, I noticed, was the last date to mail out the checks for the monthly bills without a penalty. The ache behind my eyes flared into full size pain. We used to do the budget and the bills together, I remembered. One more job my husband had dumped on me! Why had I ever married him? How could I ever have thought I loved him? When he was so selfish and so terribly thoughtless?

Isn't that paragraph monotonous? I'm afraid you may decide to quit reading before you get to the end. Now, let's break it up.

His lips pressed in a thin, tight line, he slammed the door and stamped off to work.

Drooping with the weight of my anger, I added the breakfast dishes to the pile in the sink. I ought to clean the kitchen, I thought. I looked with dull eyes at the toast crumbs under the table and the sticky circle of orange juice spilled in front of the refrigerator. Even the calendar hung at a crooked angle.

Today, I noticed, was the last date to mail out bills without a penalty.

The ache behind my eyes flared into full size pain. We used to do the budget and the bills together, I remembered. One more job my husband had dumped on me!

Why had I ever married him? How could I ever have thought I loved him when he was so selfish and so terribly thoughtless?

"Try a Love Account" by Fanny-Maude Evans,
Lady's Circle, September, 1975

See how dividing that block of print helps to keep you interested? Only one long paragraph with the others short encourages you to keep traveling down the page.

Long or short, each paragraph should serve a purpose. It should help the reader in some way. Sometimes it moves the story forward. Let's look at paragraphs in the South Seas story again.

The motor bellowed above the surf but the boat swirled sideways. Washed back. Powerless. Helpless in the grip of the sea.

This short paragraph moves us closer and closer to danger.

Occasionally, just one paragraph can help you understand a character.

Trev planted his feet wide apart, balancing against the roll of the yacht. Brushing tanned fingers through sun-bleached hair, he squinted out at the open water, his blue eyes reflecting its turbulence. Though only sixteen, he'd already proved he could handle boats on this, his first trip to Polynesia.

Can't you see this boy balancing in the boat?

Some paragraphs help to show you the scene clearly.

Trev hunched his shoulders. He looked down at the shore-boat, its white paint streaked and faded. Tied to the landing steps, it bounced and swayed to the hard rock beat of an ocean high on wind and rain. As it settled into a trough the boy grabbed a coffee can and began to bail.

Often, a paragraph can help your reader to share your feelings.

Though the tropic sun beat against my back, I shivered as I looked up. Pushing out of the bay, grotesque rock towers and pinnacles reared above me. Their black shadows crept like manacing fingers down to join the crashing waves. I shivered again, for they reminded me of the dark shadows hanging over the cruise.

No matter what their purpose or length, paragraphs need to connect smoothly with each other. As we move from one to the other we need transitions to ease the bumps. They urge us on and move us forward. Often a single word like *now* will blend one paragraph into another.

Trev's fellow crew members muttered and complained about the extra work. When the boy did not join in, they called him that "dumb smart aleck kid".
Now, he straightened up and steadied the boat. He said nothing as the first mate and engineer climbed in. Bolstering their courage with cans of beer, they ignored the boy as he bent over to start the motor.

See how the word *now* leads you from the end of the first paragraph into the second? You'll find dozens more transition words. *Although, certainly, however, inevitably, instead, naturally, nevertheless, usually, yet* are a few. And did you once learn that you never begin a sentence with *and* or *but?* That's another rule to forget. Add *and* and *but* to your list of transition words. You'll find them useful.

Watch, though, that you don't write any transition word too often. When I was a beginning writer, I submitted a story for criticism. The teacher wrote on my paper, "A fine piece but you 'butted' me to death." I counted sixteen *buts* in that story.

Sometimes a clause or a phrase will help one paragraph flow into another.

Trev pulled the starter cord. The engine stuttered. He pulled again. It coughed, then roared. Bucking against the sea, they plunged toward the open water.

Running beyond the line of foam, the boy guided them past the blowhole shooting out like a geyser.

See how smoothly the phrase "running beyond the line of foam" takes you from the preceding paragraph into the new one. And notice the clause that links these two paragraphs:

In the late 1800's the Royal Society of London set up a committee to study color-blindness. As a result, they recommended that people applying for railroad positions or seagoing jobs should take color-vision tests.

When my husband realized he couldn't be a railroad engineer or ship's officer, he specialized in electronics. Ignoring the color codes, he memorized hundreds of electrical circuits.

The clause "When my husband realized he couldn't be a railroad engineer or ship's officer" connects easily with the previous paragraph.

Besides clauses and phrases, you can use time words to join paragraphs. *Last year, that day, the next morning, years later* or *years before, then, afterward, eventually, soon, meanwhile, sometimes, always, earlier,* each moves you backward or forward.

Then, just when I was really beginning to believe I could succeed at my job, my whole world fell apart.

For months I'd had a twinge in my right side. At first I tried to ignore it. But it developed into a sharp knife-thrust pain. My leg stiffened. Each day I limped more and more back and forth from my desk to my files, holding onto chairs, shelves or anything else I could grab to steady me.

Eventually, when I could stand it no longer, I made an appointment to see a doctor.

Do you see how the words *Then, for months,* and *eventually* take readers back and bring them forward in the story?

You can bridge paragraphs, too, with an echo. Repeat a key word or words from the preceding paragraph to begin the new one.

Poor Kathy, I thought, as I poured her a cup of coffee. She needs a love account.

It hadn't been so long since I'd needed a love account myself.

The words *love account* echo to connect the two paragraphs.

Another way to move from one paragraph to the next is to leapfrog. Remember in Chapter 11 how you skipped over unimportant details? You can do the same thing between paragraphs. In a story about Hawaii's little elves, I leapfrogged to take us from midnight to dawn.

Just after midnight high up on the slopes of Kauai's Mount Waileale, a Honolulu ornithologist jerked awake. Tired out from searching for the rare O'o'a'a' bird, he'd crawled into a cave to rest.

A thud sounded from the trail outside.

"HallOO!" the ornithologist called.

Only his own voice echoed and re-echoed in the darkness.

At dawn, he looked down at new stones laid in the mountain path.

"The Conscientious Elves of Hawaii" by Fanny-Maude Evans, *Passages,* November, 1974

I didn't have to tell you that the ornithologist went back to the cave and slept until morning. You assume that he did but it's not important to the story.

Occasionally, to link paragraphs, you can ask a question in one and answer it in the next.

Look at these two paragraphs in the color-blind story:

And what about driving? How can Paul possibly interpret the traffic signals?

"No problem," he insists. "Green is brighter. Besides, the red is always on top."

As you read, this week, watch for transitions. You'll probably find all types. See how many different kinds writers use to carry their paragraphs along. And, if your own writing seems rough and jerky, check your transitions. Maybe you need to flatten the bumps between your paragraphs with transition clauses, phrases, and words. Look at your paragraphs, too. Are they mostly long and drawn out or short and choppy?

Give us some of each so we won't fall asleep as we travel along your memoir road.

19

Sentences That Speed Your Journey

As you travel through your paragraphs, your sentences help to set your speed. They slow it down or speed it up. A sentence generally is a group of words with a subject and a predicate. Yet it may be only one word like "Halt!" with the subject understood. Or it can be a fragment of a sentence for emphasis.

I could feel the water creeping up. And up. Coiling around my legs.

Just as you ride in different-model cars, your sentences have different forms. Some are simple, with the action moving in a straight line:

I remember the Depression.

Simple sentences with ideas that go together become compound when connected by words like *and, but, or.*

I remember the Depression but I don't want to write about it.

Others have a clause or two hooked on to make them complex.

Although I remember the Depression, I don't want to write about it.

No matter what type of sentence you write, you must be sure your reader understands what you are saying. Like the windows of your car, your sentences should be clean and clear. Each should have only one main idea.

What's wrong with this sentence?

When I read that book I thought it was exceptional and I have read other books like it.

It has two main ideas, doesn't it? To change it, you might make it a complex sentence.

Even though I have read other books like it, I thought that book was exceptional.

And how long should a sentence be? Usually the shorter the better. James Kilpatrick, writing in his nationally syndicated column on advice to writers, says, "Beware of long sentences; they spread roots that tend to trip the reader up. The period key lies nicely on the bottom row of your machine. Use it. Use it often."

But look at Faulkner, you may say, with his stretched-out sentences. When I mentioned his name to a writer friend, she replied, "I can't read him at all. I lose track of his thought in those whole-page sentences."

Long sentences lose readers. Look at this collection.

Again we were on our way, past scores of mud huts, some with grass-thatched roofs, some more elaborately finished with tile, and a few with board shutters in place of windows. In front we could see the inevitable collection of mongrel dogs, nimble goats and scrawny chickens, mingling with an assortment of children, the little boys dressed only in tiny shirts ending at the waistline. On we went past busy women kneeling at the little streams and beating the Monday's wash on the rocks, little pools of suds swirling slowly in a widening circle out from the bank.

Studies have shown that nineteen words are about as many as you can absorb in one sentence. The shortest in that paragraph has thirty-one.

Now, let's revise those sentences. Make them short.

Again we were on our way. We passed scores of mud huts. Some had grass-thatched roofs. Some were more elaborately finished with tile. A few had board shutters in place of windows. In front we could see the inevitable collection of mongrel dogs. They mingled with nimble goats and scrawny chickens. There was an assortment of children, too. The little boys were dressed only in tiny shirts. They ended at the waistline. On we went past busy women. They knelt at the little streams. They were beating the Monday's wash on the rocks. Little pools of suds swirled slowly. They widened in a circle out from the bank.

This sounds choppy, doesn't it? And it's hard to read. Maybe Hemingway could get away with it, but most of us can't. Too many short sentences become monotonous. Just as you vary paragraph length, you must vary the length of your sentences. Make many of them short but add a longer one now and then. And change your sentence patterns. Use some simple, some complex, and some compound.

Let's revise the paragraph again.

Again we were on our way past scores of mud huts. Some had grass-thatched roofs and some were elaborately finished with tile. A few had board shutters in place of windows. In front we could see the inevitable collection of mongrel dogs, nimble goats, and scrawny chickens. They mingled with an assortment of children, the little boys dressed only in tiny shirts ending at the waistline. On we went, past busy women. Kneeling at the little streams, they beat the Monday's wash on the rocks, while little pools of suds swirled slowly in a widening circle out from the bank.

It's much easier to read, isn't it?

Be careful with words in a series, too. They must match, nouns with nouns, verbs with verbs, adjectives with adjectives, and adverbs with adverbs.

Her work included cleaning, washing, and to cook the dinner.

You need to read this only once to see that *to cook the dinner* doesn't belong with the nouns *cleaning* and *washing*. Change it to:

Her work included cleaning, washing, and cooking the dinner.

Here's another sentence that doesn't match.

Jim considered his housekeeper attractive, pleasant, and knew how to make him comfortable.

That's terrible, isn't it? Rewrite it.

Jim considered his housekeeper attractive, pleasant, and skillful in making him comfortable.

Now look at adverbs.

They climbed quickly and with courage up the cliff.

With courage jars as you read. It doesn't go with the adverb *quickly*.

They climbed quickly and courageously up the cliff.

It sounds much better when quickly and courageously are parallel.

See that verb forms in a series match, too.

My brother picked the tomatoes, packed them in cartons, and they were sold at the market.

Were sold doesn't go with *picked* and *packed.* Change it to:

My brother picked the tomatoes, packed them in cartons, and sold them at the market.

Watch out, too, for twisted meanings. Some of the best laughs I've had came from reading words and phrases attached to the wrong subject. Writers Jacques Barzun and Henry F. Graff give us a classic textbook example in their book *The Modern Researcher.*

The wind blew across the desert where the corpse lay and whistled.

You laugh because you know corpses don't whistle. If you look again you see that the word *whistled* is out of place. There are several ways to change it. The simplest is:

The wind blew and whistled across the desert where the corpse lay.

But this doesn't put the emphasis in the right place. The authors finally change it to:

Across the desert where the corpse lay, the wind blew and whistled.

Newspapers are sources of priceless misplaced modifiers.

She waved as she drove past some 50,000 people in a yellow limousine.

Lost: Small black dog, cocker type, elderly lady attached.

The police killed a man with an ax.

How would you change these sentences to make them say what they mean?

The yellow limousine belongs to the subject *she.*

Driving a yellow limousine, she waved as she passed 50,000 people.

We know that the elderly lady was attached to the dog emotionally, not literally. Let's make it clear.

Lost by heartbroken elderly lady: Small black dog, cocker type.

And the ax refers to the man, not the police.

The police killed a man who was attacking with an ax.

Often we create these mix-ups and danglers because we separate a word from its modifier or leave the subject out entirely.

He is the product of alcoholic parents and orphanages who ran away from home eight times.

Who ran away from home eight times? Alcoholic parents and orphanages? Of course not. *He* ran away from home. Let's put the clause in the right place.

The product of alcoholic parents and orphanages, he ran away from home eight times.

And can you imagine the Washington Monument doing this?

Walking down the street, the Washington Monument seemed to tower over everything.

We know the Washington Monument wasn't walking down the street. Who was?

Walking down the street, I thought the Washington Monument seemed to tower over everything.

Besides keeping your modifiers in order, you may want to emphasize some part of your sentence. How? Put the most important words at the end.

She lost her job since she always came late.

This sentence emphasizes the fact that she always came late, but the important words are that she lost her job.

Since she always came late, she lost her job.

Here's another sentence that needs a change of emphasis.

She crept into the haunted house though she was afraid.

Here the fact that she crept into the haunted house is more important than that she was afraid, isn't it?

Though she was afraid, she crept into the haunted house.

Now, read your sentences aloud to find out where the emphasis should go. Check your modifiers, too. Are they in the right place? Do any of your sentences have more than one main idea? Look carefully at each one. Shorten or lengthen those that need it. Speed them up or slow them down to make our trip through your memory lane a pleasant one.

For practice, revise these sentences. Rewrite those with unrelated ideas, choppiness, mismatched words, misplaced modifiers, or emphasis in the wrong place.

1. Bob is lazy and he studies math.
2. He said the man lied and he met him on the bus.
3. My brother played basketball in high school and he didn't go to college.

4. The money was in the drawer. My mother threw it there. The burglar found it.
5. My father didn't like brown. His new suit was brown.
6. We bought a Buick. The Buick was blue. I like a blue car.
7. Using the microphone the candidate's speech came across well.
8. Ringing the bell, the door opened.
9. He interviewed addicts at a clinic that had suffered a drug overdose.
10. I like baseball, football, and to jog.
11. My sister has big eyes, rosy cheeks, and she smiles a lot.
12. The neighbor boy broke the window, climbed in, and had soon eaten the cookies.
13. The house burned down even though we fought the fire.
14. We were half-frozen and tired from our trip.
15. The bear attacked the child although she ran around the corner.

20

Road Signs and Traffic
Signals — Punctuation

Just as our title says, punctuation marks are the road signs and traffic signals that guide us on our journey through your memoirs. Just think of the chaos there would be on a freeway or busy intersection without any traffic signs or signals. You wouldn't know when to slow down, speed up, change lanes, or stop. If you left out punctuation marks in your writing, your readers would have the same feeling of confusion.

Greek and Latin manuscripts that have come down to us in their original form are almost impossible to read. They have no punctuation and no breaks between words. If Ella Wheeler Wilcox had written like that, could you read it?

Laughandtheworldlaughswithyouweepandyouweepalone

Today, though we have punctuation, we have a different problem. Writers, teachers, and editors disagree on what is correct. Some still use what we call *close punctuation*, laden with commas, colons, and semicolons.

We thought the story was, for the most part, false; the teacher thought so, as well.

Other authorities prefer open punctuation, using few commas, colons, or semicolons.

We thought the story was for the most part false and the teacher thought so as well.

About all that the experts do agree on is the use of a period or question mark at the end of a sentence.

It's up to you to use your own common sense. Remember your purpose—to help us understand. Listen to your writing. Be sure your punctuation makes clear what you meant to say.

Robert Ripley once told of a Russian ruler who was asked to pardon captured soldiers. He wrote this message, "Pardon impossible, to be sent to Siberia."

But the messenger, sympathizing with the soldiers, moved the comma. The message now read, "Pardon, impossible to be sent to Siberia."

I'm sure you're not in danger of going to Siberia, with or without a comma. But you do need to know what punctuation to use. No punctuation at all within a sentence is like a green light. It means "keep going."

On the wall behind us a waterfall painted on a scroll splashed down from a pine-dotted mountain.

A yellow light warns you to slow down. And that is what a comma, semicolon, colon, or dash does.

The comma signals the shortest pause of all. Many writers today use few commas. Yet, like the Russian ruler, we need them sometimes to make our meaning clear. In this short sentence, see what a comma does.

Do you remember John?
Do you remember, John?

The comma changes the meaning completely.

Of course, though, you use commas in a series of three or more words, phrases, or clauses. Before the *and,* you can add the comma or leave it out.

I like stories about travel, adventure, and romance.
I like stories about travel, adventure and romance.

We drove to the mountains, rented a cabin, and spent the night.
We drove to the mountains, rented a cabin and spent the night.

You need a comma, too, to set off introductory words, phrases, or dependent clauses.

However, we do plan to attend the play.
In spite of the weather, we plan to attend the play.
Even though the weather is bad, we plan to attend the play.

You can take your choice about using a comma before *and, but, or, for* when they join two independent clauses. If the clauses are long, use the comma.

She was worried about the boy, and I promised to phone her when he arrived.
She was worried about the boy and I promised to phone her when he arrived.

The class began with thirty students, but within a week only half remained.
The class began with thirty students but within a week only half remained.

The mechanic said the car might be out of gas, or the battery might be down.
The mechanic said the car might be out of gas or the battery might be down.

Cheerful people are fun to be with, for happiness is contagious.
Cheerful people are fun to be with for happiness is contagious.

In very short sentences leave the comma out.

The lion roared and the tiger paced.

Leave it out, too, if you can't tell whether you need a comma or not. Read your story aloud. If you come to a sentence like this, you'll know you need one.

When we cooked the girl in the next apartment said we used too much garlic.

Obviously you are not a cannibal. Add a comma after cooked.

Use commas to set off *nonrestrictive* clauses and phrases, ones that merely add extra information to a sentence and are not necessary to make the meaning clear.

The cars, a Buick and a Mercedes, collided on the corner and were demolished.

In this sentence *the cars* collided on the corner and *were demolished* is the important fact. *A Buick and a Mercedes* is just added information.

Do not use commas, though, to enclose *restrictive* clauses and phrases, those necessary to give meaning to the sentence.

The cars that collided on the corner were demolished.

Here *that collided on the corner* identifies the particular cars.

The semicolon, like the comma, is a yellow light but it holds for a longer time. It has a slightly Victorian flavor, and we do not see it as often today as we once did. You can use a semicolon between two long independent clauses that are not joined by a conjunction, are too different to be joined by a comma, or are too similar to be individual sentences.

The house was old, with a sagging roof, creaking doors and rusty hinges; but it still took me back to my childhood.

I entertain by playing the piano; Martha entertains with dramatic skits.

If we went to church, we were fanatics; if we stayed home, we were sinners.

Use the semicolon sparingly. Generally, you can make two sentences instead.

The colon, another warning of a brief pause, is even more outdated than the semicolon. Yet it can be useful. It tells you to slow down and get ready for something to come. It explains or expands on the statement preceding it. And it may introduce a list of items set off from the rest of the sentence.

I need certain qualities in a secretary: efficiency, courtesy, intelligence, and dependability.

Capitalize the word following a colon only if it is a complete sentence.

There is just one thing I can promise you about this program: It will cost you less.

The dash slows you down for an abrupt change in the direction your sentence is going. Today it is much overused.

Will we—can we—make that deadline?

It sometimes takes the place of a comma or of a colon.

Here is my explanation—but you won't like it.

You can use a dash for emphasis.

I was pleased—delighted, I should say—with my grade.

Notice that you use dashes both before and after a phrase in the middle of your sentence.

Remember that the dash is only one kind of yellow light. Use it sparingly.

The red light, of course, warns you to come to a full stop. Periods, question marks, and exclamation points are punctuation's red lights.

Use periods to mark the ends of statements.

Shivering, I sank into semidarkness. Shadowy figures came and went. Evening faded into night.

Three periods (. . .) indicate that something is left out in a quotation.

I always intended, as the teacher suggested, to read my writing aloud.
I always intended . . . to read my writing aloud.

Use four periods (. . . .) when something is omitted at the end of a quoted sentence.

If you look at your work to admire it, you are lost, for it will be like admiring your reflection in a mirror.
If you look at your work to admire it, you are lost. . . .

I'm sure you know that you use a question mark after a question.

Where will we be going tomorrow?

But be sure you do *not* use a question mark after an indirect question.

She asked where we would be going tomorrow.

The exclamation point is an oversize red light. In newsrooms it's sometimes called a "screamer." And that's what it does—it screams and yells. Try to make your words, rather than the exclamation point, express your strong emotion. You may be tempted to write sentences like these:

At last! I had bought the red convertible!

Why not really show us your feelings?

For months, each time I had passed the dealer's show window I had stopped to stare at the shiny red car. I had wished and hoped and dreamed that someday I would sit in the driver's seat. Now at last, that dream had come true. I had bought the red convertible.

Of course, there are times when you really want to scream or yell. Then you use an exclamation point.

"Blast you!" he yelled. "Get out of this house!"

And notice apostrophes. In a cartoon in our local paper a little girl says to her brother, "You forgot to put a catastrophe in *don't.*"

An apostrophe can be a catastrophe if you misplace it or forget it when you need it. To show possession, it's easy to add *'s* to nouns not ending in *s*.

That man's fishing pole is the best.
Those women's dresses are the most expensive.

But you get into trouble when you have to add 's to nouns ending with s. If the word is plural you have no problem. Add only the apostrophe.

The boys' fishing poles were stolen.

Authorities disagree about a singular noun ending with s. William Strunk, Jr., and E. B. White, authors of *Elements of Style*, say you must add both the apostrophe and the s. Other authorities add only an apostrophe.

I borrowed James's book.
I borrowed James' book.

If you are confused, add the 's. Most authorities will agree with you.

In contractions, use an apostrophe to show that a letter or letters have been left out.

They are going to enjoy the tour.
They're going to enjoy the tour.

Please do not make so much noise.
Please don't make so much noise.

Use an apostrophe to show that a number has been omitted, too.

She left college in the winter of 1946.
She left college in the winter of '46.

One warning: Be careful of *its*. Many people seem to confuse *its*, showing possession, with *it's*, the contraction for *it is*.

The sky is beautiful. Its colors fairly glow. It's a beautiful, glowing sky.

All this about punctuation may seem more trouble than it's worth. Don't worry about it. Read your writing aloud. Put your punctuation where you pause, take a breath, or stop. Be sure it makes sense. Whether you choose open or close punctuation, be consistent. Just remember you are installing traffic lights and signs to guide us through your memoirs.

21

Write in Style—Your Own

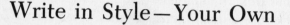

By now many of your friends know you are writing your memoirs. One, who is a writer, asks, "What style are you using?"

You gulp and stutter, for you don't really know. What is style, anyway? And should you worry about it?

There is no really satisfactory explanation of style. Style is what you say and how you say it. It's the way you put words on paper. It's as much a part of you as your speech.

For example, all of your life you have called Aunt Susie "Aunt," pronounced like the word "ant." Abruptly you decide you've been wrong. You say "Aunt" as in "haunt" or as in "want." Your friends will smile and perhaps accuse you of putting on airs. Aunt Susie may even refuse to answer. Your new pronunciation sounds artificial because it's not you.

So it is with your writing. Just as your style of dress tells us something about you, your style of writing reflects your personality. If you try to copy someone else, your style will seem as synthetic as a plastic geranium. It's tempting to imitate favorite authors, writers whose way with words you especially admire. Of course you can learn from them. Notice figures of speech, phrases, special descriptions. Consciously and subconsciously your reading will influence your style.

Sometimes, just for fun, try to copy the way a writer you like puts words together. But in your own writing, be yourself. Don't be like a student Faulkner once had. After reading his manuscript, the famous writer said, "Your writing sounds more like me than I do."

Don't compare your stories with those of anyone else, either. Sometimes I hear a student say, "I'm discouraged. I can't write the way she does. The people in her memoirs are so real I feel I know them. Mine seem like zombies."

Or another says, "I wish I had his talent. Everything he writes is so funny. But when I try humor it just sounds silly."

Of course some of you will write more easily and fluently than others. Yet only you can tell your stories. Only you have had your experiences, and the way you tell them is your own.

Your style helps your reader to know you. It shows your tastes, standards, and preferences. It is so much a part of a writer that often you can recognize an author before you see his name. Look at these two descriptions of spring flowers.

> I wander'd lonely as a cloud
>   That floats on high o'er vales and hills,
> When all at once I saw a crowd,
>   A host, of golden daffodils;
> Beside the lake, beneath the trees,
>   Fluttering and dancing in the breeze.

"The Daffodils" by William Wordsworth

> In the dooryard fronting an old farm-house near
>   the whitewash'd palings,
> Stands the lilac-bush tall-growing with
>   heart-shaped leaves of rich green,

With many a pointed blossom rising delicate, with the
perfume strong I love.

"When Lilacs Last in the Dooryard Bloom'd" by Walt Whitman

Each of these poets is speaking in his own voice, giving
us a picture of daffodils and lilacs, but each in a very
different style. If Wordsworth were writing about lilacs,
he would perhaps have them nodding and waltzing in the
breeze. While Whitman, writing about daffodils, might
mention their cup-shaped blossoms and spiky leaves.

We can often recognize students' writing, too, by their
style. These students are all writing about a storm but
notice how different each piece is.

Father was afraid of lightning and passed his fear on to his
children. Never use a telephone during a storm! Never stand by
a window! About the only thing he considered safe was to close
one's eyes and pray. And pray hard!

We lived in a prairie town where we could see storms approaching long before they struck. Father would hurry home—
to scare us. One particularly bad storm happened in the evening. Thunder cracked and lightning lit up the sky. A bolt
struck a transformer just outside our home, and the lights went
out. My sister and I had had enough of the storm and raced for
our bedroom. As we plunged into bed, from opposite sides, our
heads met with a crash. We were sure we had been struck by
lightning.

Esther Clifton

A sudden chill settled over the town. Off to the west, a green-
ish-black sky carried a strong foreboding of hail.

An aura of worry settled over the wheat-belt town of McDon-
ald, Kansas. Acre upon acre of wheat stood tall in the fields,
heavy heads rippling in the breeze. Harvest very soon, if hail
didn't knock the golden stalks to the ground.

A tentative shower of hail set in. The ground turned white but the stones were small and wouldn't do much damage. Then a heavier onslaught burst down.

I thought of thousands of acres of wheat surrounding the town.

I thought of the farmers and townspeople depending upon the harvest.

I crossed my fingers.

R. A. Vanderlippe

Summer thunderstorms are great. They excite me. I love the wild moments of the fresh-smelling wind, forerunner of the rain to come, when whitecaps suddenly appear on the lake and the boats tied at the docks start to plunge up and down like rocking horses. Then the trees along the shore bend, and sand and leaves and pine needles and tiny birch branches sail through the air, making a tattoo on our closed windows. The sky grows rapidly darker as a huge cloud oozes shoreward to the accompaniment of, first, a rumble and, finally, the jolting crashes of thunder. Lightning pierces the sky. The big raindrops have given way to a solid curtain of rain marching across the water, smoothing the wild waves. The storm is in full sway. I love it.

K. Shelley

The stars had been shining bright in the dark November sky that year of 1958 when a strong gust of wind hit the west side of my house. The house moaned as the wind passed by. The next gust caused the electricity to go off. We had an oil heater in the dining room, so I shut it off for fear of an explosion. I dug out candles and lit the kerosene lamp. Because of my concern my son became frightened. I tucked him into bed against the strongest wall and lay down until he fell asleep. I waited for the storm to pass but time seemed to creep as the wind became more violent. The house began to breathe during each blast, the walls to heave in the center. Then as if it were tired of holding its breath, the house would let out a sigh, allowing the strain of the wind to pass from its insides. A vacuum filled the rooms and I prayed my home would survive this onslaught of nature. From 6:15 to 10:00 P.M., when the storm receded, the countryside was relentlessly beaten by 140-mile-per-hour winds and rain.

Dahl C. Phelps

Do you always write in the same way or can you change your style?

Writers can vary their way of writing to suit their subject. Certainly you would not want to write about a sad experience such as a funeral in the same joyful style as you would use to describe a wedding. Yet the way you use words and phrases will identify the writing as yours. Your style will change only when you change. As an adult you no longer think and talk as you did in your teens. So your style of writing will mature. The image it reflects will match the person you have become. Of course, you can improve it, just as you can improve the way you speak. A good style guide is that small book *The Elements of Style* by William Strunk, Jr., and E. B. White. Many of the points they make we have studied in earlier chapters.

As we've emphasized, you should write naturally and read your work aloud to listen to its rhythm. Remember, you should have some kind of plan and a guideline to point the way on your writing map.

Strong nouns and verbs are more vivid than adjectives and adverbs. And sentences should be short rather than long. Do you use repetition? It can be good or bad. Check it in your writing. Throw it out if it has crept in without your knowing. And, of course, you'll watch clutter. Have you weeded out dropout words and clichés?

What about the people in your stories? Can we see

them as real persons and hear them speak? Or are they still stick figures? Do you help us to taste, touch, smell, and hear as well as see your descriptions? Can we really share your feelings? Keep us wondering, too, what's going to happen. And, on that last page, chop off your writing at a spot that satisfies.

Above all, don't worry about your style. You are painting a picture with words. Just as in painting with oils or watercolors, you decide on the outline, choose the details, and select the shades. You can study and practice and improve. But write as you speak, with your own voice. For your style is you.

22

Analyze to Realize

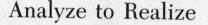

That word *analyze* may sound a little scary. Why and what do you need to analyze? And how do you do it?

You may not know it but you already make an analysis of everything you read. You turn the last page and say, "That was great. I loved that story." Or you throw down the piece before you've even finished it and groan, "I could do better."

And that's the reason you need to take time to analyze what you read, to take a close look at the various parts. You can improve your own writing by finding out what is good or bad in the books and magazines you read. Learn what captures your interest or what puts you to sleep.

Let's look at a published article. You've seen some parts of it in other chapters, but now read the entire piece.

The Magic Map

A map can be a traveler's best friend, indispensable for locating roads, rivers and restaurants. But it can be more: it can have a touch of magic.

My husband and I discovered this special quality on our own self-guided tour around the world. Arriving at the airport in Auckland, New Zealand, we picked up a packet of maps and sat down to locate the tourist rooms where we planned to stay. A stocky young man strung with cameras plopped down beside us.

"May I help?" he asked, pointing to our map.

We told him the address we wanted. He pulled out a pencil and traced our route along a major avenue. Handing us his card, he gave us a warm invitation to call him when we visited Christchurch, where he lived.

Later, when we reached that city, we phoned him rather hesitantly. He and his wife rushed over in their car to give us a deluxe tour. As a teacher, he could not only show us the local sights but add bonus bits of history, too. We ended the day with dinner at their home and a taste of New Zealand kiwi fruit.

The friendly couple offered, too, to take us to the airport when we left.

Even in bustling Tokyo the magic continued. On a frosty winter afternoon we shivered on a corner while we studied our city map till our eyes ached. Where in the world was the consul's office?

A Japanese man in a business suit hurried toward us and almost slid to a stop. With a polite bow he offered to help. He glanced at the map.

"Too far," he said. "Too many subway. Come, I show you."

At the station he bought our tickets, handed them to us with another bow and smiled a refusal when we tried to pay. When our car came, we turned to thank him but he followed us aboard. At stop after stop we expected to see him get off, but he sat in his seat, his hands folded over his briefcase, until we reached our destination. Then, with a final bow, he crossed over the tracks to take a return car.

On the other side of the world the map still worked its wonders. In Paris, we lost our hotel on a rainy day. As we stopped to spread the map against an old stone building, two Frenchwomen stopped too. When they saw the written address, they frowned at the map, chattering to each other. Motioning to us to come, they took off down the street. We followed them for blocks until they walked right up to our hotel lobby. They shook the water from their umbrellas, smiled and hurried down the boulevard before we could so much as offer a cup of coffee.

In Spain, we were lost once more after taking a detour on a narrow dirt road. Pulling over beside an orange grove, we unfolded the map across the steering wheel.

A young man with a farmer's tan vaulted over the fence to lean on our car window. We traced the dark line of the highway and, in primitive Spanish, asked how to find it. The man scowled at the map. He ran back to the orchard, grabbed up a sack of oranges and tossed them into our car. Was our Spanish that bad? Had we mixed up highways and oranges?

But the farmer pushed a motorbike out from behind a shed, jumped on and roared down the road, waving to us to follow. Kilometer after kilometer we twisted and turned around hairpin curves until at last we came to the highway. With a smart salute the young Spaniard sped away.

In Germany the map worked its greatest magic of all. We felt like prisoners in the maze of Bremen's city streets—no matter which one we followed, it always brought us back to the square. Around and around we went, searching for a way out. Back at the square once more, we parked in a no parking zone and pulled out our map.

Almost as if he had been waiting for us, a policeman popped up beside the car. We shuddered. What was the penalty in Germany for illegal parking? A ticket and a fine? Or jail? And what were German jails like?

But the policeman said in perfect English, "May I please be of help?"

Taking a deep breath, I explained. He looked at the map and shook his head. "It's very difficult. It's better that I show you."

He climbed in beside us and guided us carefully down one street and up another for more than two miles. At last he asked us to stop.

"Go straight," he said. "Your road is ahead."

"But how will you get back?" we asked.

He hunched a shoulder. "Walk. It's not far." Touching his cap, he strode off.

And so it went. In every country the magic led us to our destinations. But it did more. It overcame the language barrier and introduced us to the people, as well as the places, of other nations.

Fanny-Maude Evans, Odyssey, March-April, 1981

Let's see how I put this story together. What about the title? Remember, it should attract attention, above all. This topic title would have little appeal without that word *magic*. I doubt that you would read anything titled "The Map," but adding that one word makes you want to read on.

Is there a plan? If you've read carefully, you've found that the plan is the list—the simplest way of all to put your writing together. All the different incidents when the map became a best friend make up the list.

And what about the beginning? Read the first paragraph again.

A map can be a traveler's best friend, indispensable for locating roads, rivers and restaurants.

This first sentence gives you an idea you may not have thought of—that a map can be a traveler's best friend.

But it can be more: it can have a touch of magic.

Here you have the guideline that tells you where you're going in order to find out how a map can be magic.

Now go on to the second paragraph.

My husband and I discovered this special quality on our own self-guided tour around the world. Arriving at the airport in

Auckland, New Zealand, we picked up a packet of maps and sat down to locate the tourist rooms where we planned to stay.

Let's see, now, if you can find the four *w*'s in these two lead paragraphs. *Who*— my husband and I. *What*— we discovered this special quality (how a map can have a touch of magic). *When*— on our own self-guided tour. *Where*— around the world. This beginning is short, two paragraphs. Yet it contains everything you need to lead you into the first experience.

Study the anecdotes. Each begins with the setting, introduces a problem, characters, action, and a solution, to complete a small story. Look at the Tokyo anecdote.

SETTING:	Even *in bustling Tokyo* the magic continued. On *a frosty winter afternoon* we shivered *on a corner.*
CHARACTERS:	*My husband* and I and *a Japanese man.*
ACTION:	We *shivered* on a corner while we *studied* our city map. A Japanese man . . . *hurried toward us* and *almost slid to a stop.* With a *polite bow* he *offered to help.* He *glanced at the map* . . . he *bought our tickets, handed them to us with another bow* . . . *smiled a refusal* . . . *we tried to pay* . . . we *turned to thank him* but he *followed us aboard* . . . he *sat in his seat* . . . *with a final bow, he crossed over the tracks* to *take a return car.*
PROBLEM SOLUTION:	We reached our destination.

Now let's look at the characters more closely. You can see us shivering on a corner, trying to pay for the tickets and to thank the Japanese man, and watching for him to get off. But the main character is the Japanese man. In only a few words he becomes a real person. We see him wearing a business suit, stopping, bowing, offering to help. We see him riding with his hands folded over his briefcase and bowing as he exits.

In this anecdote and the others in this particular story there's not much chance for conversation since our foreign-language ability is limited. Yet we do hear the Japanese man. "Too far," he said. "Too many subway. Come, I show you."

Study the characters in the other anecdotes. Two Frenchwomen stopped, frowned at the map, chattered to each other. Motioning to us to come, they walked right up to our hotel lobby. A young man with a farmer's tan vaulted over the fence, scowled at the map, tossed oranges into our car, roared down the road, and with a smart salute sped away. Finally we see a policeman pop up, in perfect English offer to help, climb in beside us, touch his cap as he leaves to walk back. All these sentences, phrases, and verbs act like a Polaroid camera. They give us an instant picture of a person.

Look at the verbs again. *Plopped, rushed, shivered, hurried, frowned, shook, vaulted, grabbed up, roared, popped up, hunched.* They help us to see people in action, don't they?

Now let's examine the style. As you know, your style is the way you put your writing together. "The Magic Map" has an informal narrative style in a series of small stories to illustrate an experience. It's appropriate to this kind of writing. Notice how each anecdote leads into another, with interest rising to the climax. Look at the sentences and paragraphs. You'll find some long and some short for variety. Read the piece aloud to find out if the paragraphs flow smoothly from one to another with good transitions.

And what about repetition? The word *magic* is repeated four times.

But it can be more: it can have a touch of *magic*.
Even in bustling Tokyo the *magic* continued.
In Germany the map worked its greatest *magic* of all.
In every country the *magic* led us to our destinations.

This is repetition for a purpose. Each time you read *magic* it emphasizes that quality in the map.

Now, look at the ending, as you did in Chapter 6.

And so it went. In every country the magic led us to our destinations. But it did more. It overcame the language barrier and introduced us to the people, as well as the places, of other nations.

Remember how this ending echoes the word *magic?* And it adds one new observation.

It overcame the language barrier and introduced us to the people, as well as the places, of other nations.

To practice analyzing, use this check list. Find a published story you do or do not like. Read it over. Then ask and answer each question. Make sideline notes and underline.

Analyzing—Check Questions

1. Where is the article going?
2. Does it arrive?
3. Does it have a good title? What type? Does it capture your interest? How?
4. Is the form or plan appropriate for the material? What type is it?

5. Does the hook grab attention? Create suspense?
6. What is the guideline? Where do you find it?
7. How long is the lead? Does it include the four *w*'s?
8. What about anecdotes? Are they plotted with setting, problem, characters, action, and a solution? Are they short and to the point?
9. Can we see and hear the people?
10. Are the verbs strong and active?
11. What type of style? Is it suitable to the subject? Does it show rather than tell? Is repetition good or bad?
12. Do the sentences and paragraphs vary in length? Are there more short than long? Are transitions smooth?
13. Does the ending satisfy? What type is it?

Use this list to check your own writing. You'll be surprised at how much it helps you, for you'll find out what is good and what needs improving. When you analyze, you'll realize what makes a memoir a delight or turns it into drivel.

23

A Special Memoir — Sharing Your Travels

By now, no doubt, you're well along on your memory trail. As you write more and more of your life experiences, you remember special trips you'd like to share. That long, dusty wagon ride to camp out in the Rockies. The hectic drive across two states in your Model T with the engine coughing and sputtering and endless flats to change. The trip in the train with the wood-burning engine that sent a continuous shower of soot and sparks over all the passengers. Or even your first flight in a jet so gigantic you wondered if it could ever lift off the ground. All of these are exciting and vivid to you, but how do you make them interesting to others?

It sounds easy. All you have to do is tell what happened.

That's what you're tempted to do. But in writing about your travels what you leave out is much more important than what you include. You forget that today most of us have already been there or have read about or seen pictures of nearly every spot in the world.

Remember how dull an evening can be when friends invite you to see their vacation slides? They show tray after tray until you want to shut your ears as well as your eyes.

Some years ago when Russia was still closed to most outsiders, a colleague of my husband's visited that country on a special mission. He invited a crowd of us to view his slides. At first we were excited to see scenes of this novel and interesting country. But, as hour after hour passed, the chairs began to feel harder and harder. At midnight he announced, "We'll have a short break for refreshments and then go on."

As he disappeared into the kitchen, we grabbed our coats and slipped away.

Of course you don't want your travel memoir to be like that. You have to be selective. The first two or three hundred slides hold our interest. After that, they become tiresome. So it is with your writing. Choose special details. Tell us how *you* felt, what happened to *you*. Forget the travel brochure with its glowing description of the Taj Mahal, the Leaning Tower of Pisa, or Hawaii's Menehunes. We want to share your romantic feelings when you saw the Taj Mahal by moonlight, your fright when you thought you were falling from the Tower of Pisa, and the real story of the Menehunes as your guide told it.

If you kept a journal, don't just copy your entries. Go over them and select experiences that are uniquely yours. When my husband and I toured Europe by car, we stayed one night at a small fishing village on the Italian Riviera. I wrote in my journal:

Decided to turn off to Camogli, small town past Genoa. Fishing village perched on rock at bottom of Monte di Portafino. Drove through narrow street, Via Garibaldi, to opening between houses. Sign says, "1.60 meters wide. Car is too big." Our hotel perched high above us on a cliff. No way we could lug our bags up that steep path. Paul decided to drive through. I was scared and got out and walked. Less than an inch on each side, but he got through. Hotel manager nice. Speaks English. Had long conversation. Once a year Camogli has mammoth fish fry in world's largest skillets. One about 12 feet across hangs on a wall. Houses all built high on cliffs to watch sea for storms. Men fishermen or sailors. Orange-striped sailboats dot bay. Blue and purple, blue and red beach umbrellas far below. Sound of surf against rocks, hiss of waves. Hear bell from 1000-year-old church. Loud deep tone underlined by lighter note from different bell. Bells compete. See warning flash of lighthouse beacon, lights of Genoa.

Now, what in this journal entry would interest someone else? The frightening ride through the too-narrow street could make an entire story by itself, with details of the cliff and the bay and the beach. The giant frying pans and the annual fish fry would be interesting, too. You could include the sounds of the surf and churchbells.

No matter what you decide to include in your travel story, remember to use the writing techniques you have been studying. First of all, you must hook your reader. In the Camogli story, I might begin:

We climbed up and up, following the narrow road hugging the cliff as if at any moment it might fall into the harbor. Abruptly we came to a sign, "1.60 meters wide. Car is too big."

Our guideline might be next:

Paul decided to try to inch the car through the narrow opening.

Wouldn't you read on to find out just how we did reach our hotel?

And of course you'll have some kind of plan. In this story it would be chronological. But be careful. In writing just as it happened, you're in danger of including too much. Choose incidents and details that are not well known. We don't really care how you slept unless an ancient ghost suddenly appeared at the foot of your bed. And we aren't especially interested in the food you ate unless it's particularly bad, good, or different. In the story of our stay in the Japanese inn, I chose incidents about our little maid, our mistakes in eating, brushing our teeth, bathing, and using slipper etiquette, since few of my friends or relatives, at that time, had stayed in an authentic ryokan.

If you're writing about an extended trip, you might like to use the list plan as I did in "The Magic Map." Emphasize one type of experience. It might be unusual people you met, unique hotels you stayed in, or plumbing you coped with.

Ever since my experience with a bathroom in India, I've wanted to write that last one. We were delighted to find a room with a full bath. After a soothing soak in the tub, I pulled the plug. I stepped out not on to a dry floor but into a rising pool of soapy water. There was no pipe connected to the drain.

In travel memoirs, clichés can be the worst trap of all. You're tempted to write: There were fabulous scenes, magnificent buildings, luxurious surroundings, breathtaking views, impressive sights, unsurpassed beauties, historic cities, incomparable mountains, splendid theaters, excellent accommodations. I once counted the word *excellent* in a travel brochure citing the charms of a European country. It appeared eighteen times in that three-page folder.

Of course, like all clichés, these are perfectly good words, but they don't give us any definite idea. What made a scene fabulous, a building magnificent or surroundings luxurious? Here again you need to be specific. You might write:

The peak towered over the city.

We have a vague idea of a high mountain and that's all. Revise it to let us really see the peak.

The peak rose 12,000 feet above the city like some giant hand, its index finger pointing toward the clouds.

Or, in describing an Australian bus trip, you may want to add more details.

Mile after mile we bumped and bounced over unpaved roads that were barely trails. As we passed the endless forests, leaping wallabys and giant ant hills, our driver entertained us. He sang cowboy ballads, recited poetry and told jokes to relieve the monotony of the 1500-mile ride. At midnight, in the middle of nowhere, he stopped, brought out huge thermoses and offered us each coffee and cookies.

And don't forget people. All of us like to hear about the guide who led you along the trail to the New Zealand glacier, the seatmate who turned out to be a pearl diver, or the man beside you on the plane who really did make Swiss watches.

Once, traveling by train in Japan, I sat by a tiny woman in traditional kimono and obi. She politely removed a huge cloth bag from the seat to give this oversize American more room. As the train sped along the track, I took out my Japanese-English dictionary and tried to begin a conversation. At first my little seatmate looked startled. Then she smiled and held out her hand for the dictionary. As we passed it back and forth, I slowly learned that she was on her way to Tokyo to sell tiny silk coin purses she had made. Opening the large bag, she took one out. It was made of tan silk sprinkled with blue flowers and would just about hold one of our half dollars. At her train stop she pressed it into my hand, smiled, bowed, and hurried down the aisle.

Notice, too, the special characteristics of places. Each has a special flavor. It may be a Hawaiian park filled with exotic flowers and birds, a Dutch street crowded with a tangle of bicycles weaving in and out, or an English hotel in India with an army of waiters in white robes, red sashes, and gold-trimmed turbans.

Do you remember how I shared the flavor in my memoir about the Japanese inn?

We followed down the silent hall, lighted by the faint glow filtering through the shoji screens. We turned a corner, and another and another, in a kind of geometric maze. We could hear only the trickle of the stream, the pad of the maid's feet and the swish of our bag along the floor. We met no one. And we didn't speak as we walked softly into this oasis of peace and quiet and solitude.

I could have written:

As we walked along the silent hall, the inn felt quiet and peaceful.

That wouldn't give you any real feeling of its peace and solitude, would it? You need not only to see but to hear, feel, taste, smell.

On a visit to Iguassú Falls in southern Brazil some years ago, I remember the taste of dust rising in clouds from the unpaved road, the mighty roar of the falls, the sight of their unique horseshoe shape, the splash of the spray on our faces, the smell of dampness and some unknown flower.

Maybe, now, though, you're saying you've never visited strange places and foreign countries. You don't have to. A shorter trip, perhaps no farther away than a lake or a park, can be just as interesting. If you lived in snow country, it might be a sleigh ride in a blizzard to attend a wedding. Or it could be a camping trip when cars had no trunks and you had to tie everything on the runningboard. You had no down sleeping bags but packed quilts and blankets and slept on a pile of pine boughs. It could be, too, your first visit to a large city with its frightening maze of streets, subways, and pedestrians.

Choose some short or long trip you would like to share. Think about it. What happened to *you?* If you've kept a journal, go over it. Pick out special incidents. Forget the travel brochures. Use them only to refresh your memory about some sight, sound, or smell you may have forgotten. Write your travel story and make it truly your own.

24

Try It Again and Again

By now your memoirs have piled up. Some have been in your drawer or on your desk for weeks and months. It's time to go back and take a fresh look at them.

All good writers revise. Gore Vidal, in an interview in the *New York Times*, says, "I am an obsessive rewriter, doing one draft and then another and another, usually five. In a way, I have nothing to say, but a great deal to add."

You probably won't want to revise your work five times. But do go over it once or twice, after you have put it away for a while. Read it aloud or tape it and listen for the overall effect. Is it interesting? Does it say what you meant to say? Use the analyzing check list you studied in Chapter 22. Ask and answer each question.

When you have checked each point, pick up your red or green pencil and go back over your work. Look with a critical eye at each sentence. Did you find clutter clogging their flow? Strike it out. "If in doubt, leave it out" is still a good motto.

Let's review some of the ways you might clutter your work. For instance, did you write:

His trip had been an exciting one.

Why not leave out the words *an* and *one?*

His trip had been exciting.

How many times have you used *who, which, that, there,* or *it?* In our lesson on clutter we discovered they were not always necessary.

Her brother *who* is older called us.
Her older brother called us.

The bulbs, *which* we planted in June, are in bloom.
The bulbs we planted in June are in bloom.

The plan *that* he had suggested was worthless.
The plan he had suggested was worthless.

There was such a crowd in the stadium we couldn't get in.
We couldn't get into the crowded stadium.

It is necessary for you to come early.
You must come early.

Look, too, at the word *very.* How many times did you use it? Does it really add to your meaning?

The boy is *very* tall and *very* strong.

Here, *very* doesn't tell us anything. Cross it out.

The boy is tall and strong.

Now we can form our own picture. Or, if you want us to know exactly how tall and how strong the boy is, tell us.

The boy is six and a half feet tall and can lift five hundred pounds.

And did you find clichés as you read your piece over? If you didn't, read it again. For, as we've learned, clichés are so much a part of our language that we don't recognize them. Did you write this sentence?

It's raining cats and dogs.

Revise it to have a fresh meaning.

Rain is gushing down like water from a broken pipeline.

And can you change some of your clauses into phrases to tighten and shorten sentences?

While he was riding on the bus, he met the president.
While on the bus, he met the president.

You know you should use adjectives and adverbs with restraint in your writing. Sometimes, though, they can be more effective than phrases.

Let's go over to the side of the street *in the shade.*
Let's go over to the *shady* side of the street.

It's important *to have a serious talk* about this.
It's important to talk *seriously* about this.

Now look again at your verbs. You've checked passive forms, but what about *to be?* Have you circled all of its forms? They don't go anywhere, you know. If possible, change them to action verbs.

My neighbor is friendly.
My neighbor smiles and says, "Hello," when we meet.

Did you forget similes and metaphors? Of course you don't want to use too many of them, but they do help us to see your picture.

The road was like a ribbon of moonlight.

or

The road was a ribbon of moonlight.

Watch for repetition. Was it conscious or unconscious? Underline words and phrases you repeated several times.

If you meant to emphasize them, fine. But if they sneaked in without your knowing it, cross them out and substitute new expressions.

When you've checked all of your sentences, look at your paragraphs. Are they in order? Do they move without a jar from one to the other? If not, use scissors and tape to rearrange them and add transitions to smooth them out.

You may want to check some of the details in your memoirs, too. How long did you live in that sod house? What color was that old buggy your grandfather rode in? How old were your parents when they were married? And how far did your father have to walk to get groceries when the roads were closed by a blizzard?

Contact your relatives who might remember. Tell them what you're doing and ask for their versions of the stories. If they don't remember the details either, then just estimate the time or distance. As to color, you'd probably be safe in saying the buggy was black or gray, or just don't mention its color at all.

Once more, read your story aloud. Are you satisfied? If not, go over it again. And again, if necessary. It seems like a lot of work. Yet you do want your memoirs to be read. The more you tighten, smooth, and polish, the more likely it is that your friends and relatives will want to read on to the end.

At some point, though, you'll feel you have revised everything enough. Stop. You don't want to polish so long and hard that you wear all the luster off. It's time, too, for you to begin thinking about how to put all those pages of memories together.

25

Wrap Up a Neat Package

You look at that box of memoir manuscripts and wonder what you will do with them. You need somehow to put them all together, whether it be in a scrapbook or a bound copy. First, though, think about illustrations—old photos, birth and death certificates, newspaper clippings of weddings, family reunions, and other special events, school reports, passports, letters—anything that relates to your stories.

One writer found a receipt dated January 8, 1898, for eleven tons of coal. The cost—$69. She decided to include it in her story about the wagon that delivered the coal in a cloud of black dust. My own grandmother had a marvelous recipe for apple crisp. What a thrill when I found it, in her spidery Victorian handwriting, in her box of recipes. It added a lot to my story about her cooking on the old black kitchen stove.

Even though you're not an artist, you can draw rough outlines of the houses, barns, or schools you have written about. Add a sketch of the floor plan. Many of us today have no idea what it's like to live in two- and three-story houses with attics and basements to explore.

And do add maps of your hometown or the places your parents and grandparents came from, if you can find them. A friend whose family originated in Poland often heard her father speak of the town of Lomza. But search as she might she could not find even a tiny village with that name on any Polish map. Leafing through an old book about Poland one day, she stopped to study one more map. To her delight, it had a tiny dot marked Lomza. She photocopied the map to add to her stories about her father.

Cut out magazine pictures, too. Today you often see artists' drawings of old stoves, antique lamps, and ancient automobiles. Use them in your memoirs.

Take pictures of buildings important to your stories, if possible. One writer made a special visit to see the New York tenement where she grew up. She spent an afternoon snapping views of the dilapidated building, while passersby stared. They thought she must be crazy but she didn't mind. Her pictures added a new dimension to her stories.

Enlist the help of your relatives. Ask them to send you old photos, documents, and records they might have. Of course, they'll want them back and you'll need to make copies. But how do you copy Aunt Mary's photo of grandmother or Uncle Jim's picture of his great-grandfather who died in the Civil War? And what about that framed record, decorated with intricate curlicues and flowers, listing birthplaces and dates for each member of your father's family?

If either you or a friend has a 35-millimeter camera with a close-up attachment, you can take pictures of such photos, records, and documents. Or you can take them to a good photocopy center. Sometimes photos come out sharper than originals, and big documents can be reduced.

Be sure, though, to shop around for the place that does

the best work for you. Try it out with a photo on a sample page to see how clear it is. Attach Aunt Mary's or Uncle John's picture to the page with pieces of double-stick adhesive tape if you might want to pull the photos up later. Or, to mount them permanently, buy Kodak's rapid mounting cement.

When you've collected your illustrations, you're ready to begin organizing all your material.

Do you have a title for your collection? If not, jot down a few ideas and play with them. One group of students decided to call their memoirs *Flashbacks* because that's what a memoir really is. Another group called theirs *Silhouettes of the Past* because a silhouette artist used her talents to illustrate it. *The Way It Was* is the title of yet another memoir book, made up of stories entered in a state contest.

You should have a title page, too. Here you might want to draw a simple family tree. You could even include a small cutout photo of each member. And you do need a table of contents. It's probably easiest to group stories alphabetically. Or you can list categories such as Adventures, Fun, In Uncle Sam's Service, Weddings I Won't Forget, Beloved Buildings.

When you've finished, read it all over and make your corrections. Then have someone else edit it for you. By this time, your mind is so familiar with the stories that it won't recognize misspelled words or faulty sentences.

At last, you're ready to do your final typing. Arrange your illustrations on the pages before you type, and mark with a pencil approximately where you want them to appear. You'll no doubt have to retype some pages, to add or subtract photos, letters, or certificates. But do try to place illustrations on every page.

Clean your typewriter keys and use a fresh ribbon so the letters will be sharp and clear. If you don't type, try to find someone in your family or a friend who would do it for you. Of course, if it's really impossible, copy your manuscript by hand rather than not at all. Perhaps later someone will type it.

Now you need to combine it all. You have a choice of several ways to do this, depending on how permanent you want your memoirs to be. One student made a fine collection by using photograph albums. She put the pictures and documents between the plastic sheets on one page and slipped her typed story into the opposite sheets. She filled several albums this way and her family enjoyed each one. You can use an album, notebook, or scrapbook, too, if you want only one copy. You may want to consider binding your book, especially when children, grandchildren and friends want copies. Most people think it costs a fortune, but many large photocopy centers also do simple binding at a reasonable rate. Shop for the best price.

Again try out a sample page. How sharp is the print? How clear are the illustrations? Some centers will collate your copies for you. But bring them all home and check them yourself. You might insert a few blank pages for adding extra notes or pictures.

If you can, bind some extra copies. You'll be surprised how many people will want them and will be willing to help out on the cost. For you are giving them a real treasure, a priceless gift that no one else can give.

Though most of you are writing for family and friends, some of you may wonder about publishing your memoirs. That is a completely different area. Entire books have been written on the subject. Before you even consider it, try to get a professional evaluation of your book. Often writing teachers, agents, or freelance writers will do this for a fee. Look, too, in writer's magazines like *Writer's Digest* or *The Writer* for criticism services. But be prepared to pay $60 to $100 or more, depending on the length of your manuscript.

If you decide to try to find a publisher, ask your librarian to suggest books that might help. Study the *Writer's Market* and the *Literary Market Place.* Also, check your local adult-education schools, colleges, and community centers for special courses offered on publishing.

All this will take time. But, if you persist, you just might possibly be that one in hundreds who finds a market for a memoir book.

26

An Unexpected Bonus

You turn the pages of your collection of memoirs and you realize that in writing them you have made new discoveries. You have found that your look at the past has been fun as well as work. And you know, now, that you have more stories to write. For, as you walked through your memory gate you found paths leading in many directions. You can fill another book and another with memoirs.

You have seen, too, that your life has been interesting. Whether you lived in the largest city or the smallest town, on a thousand-acre ranch or in a remote cabin, you have coped successfully with changes. You have lived through major wars, disasters, job changes, and technical and scientific advancements so swift they threatened to turn your world topsy-turvy. As you look back you see that you have experienced joy as well as sorrow, success as well as failure, birth as well as death. And you have met many experiences with courage and strength.

One student was surprised when she read her memoirs. "I looked back at my life," she said, "and I couldn't believe how strong I was when I faced the problems that came my way."

Something else may happen as you examine your past. Experiences that once seemed disastrous take on a new look. An educator now sees how lucky he was to lose his teaching job during the Depression. Because no other positions were available, he went back to the university and obtained a higher degree. Later, he taught in a larger school, moving up to become principal. His success there eventually brought him the position of administrator of a big metropolitan school district. He now says if he had remained in that first job, which he liked, he might still be there.

In reliving your life, you find, too, that you have been a part of some of the most important and exciting events in history. You may have experienced and observed the beginning and end of two world wars; man's first efforts to wing his way into the skies; the horseless carriage that traveled at a frightening fifteen miles per hour; the radio voices from a hundred miles away; television, bringing not only voices but pictures from across the world; the awesome advent of nuclear energy; man's walk on the moon and the beginning of the space age.

You saw and heard and felt these and other great events, and you can bring them alive for those who will only read about them in the pages of books.

You gain another bonus in reviewing the thoughts and feelings you had in the past. The way you felt will help you to understand your younger relatives, though their world may be vastly different from the one you knew. Even so, today's toddler still wants to touch, taste, smell everything he sees. A kindergartner still clutches mother's hand on that first day of school. A teenager rides an emotional roller-coaster, up one day and down the next, just as you did. And, though the words may be different, the voices of the bride and groom still tremble as they repeat their wedding vows.

A look back at the way you and your parents and grandparents met life's highlights and shadows can reassure these younger relatives. When they open the pages of the past, they will find inspiration to take each step into the future with confidence. And they will discover that they, like you, are an important link in a long ancestral chain.

Bibliography

SOURCES I HAVE USED

Sometimes you may want to learn more about a writing technique. To help you, I include this list of books I have used. Some may be out of print but you can find them at your library. Others are now in paperback and you may want to buy them.

1 Take a Look Backward

Janice T. Dixon and Dora D. Flack, *Preserving Your Past.* Doubleday, New York, 1977. Ch. I.

William J. Hoffman, *Life Writing: A Guide to Family Journals.* St. Martin's Press, New York, 1982. Chs. I, II.

Ken Macrorie, *Writing to Be Read,* revised second edition. Hayden Book Company, Rochelle Park, N.J., 1976. Ch. 1.

David Weitzman, *Underfoot.* Charles Scribner's Sons, New York, 1976. Ch. 1, pp. 13–21; Ch. 3.

2 Trigger Your Memory

William J. Hoffman, *Life Writing: A Guide to Family Journals and Personal Memoirs.* St. Martin's Press, New York, 1982. Chs. III, IV.

Society of Magazine Writers, *A Treasury of Tips for Writers* (edited by Marvin Weisbord). Writer's Digest Books, Cincinnati, 1965. Ch. 8.

3 Twice-Told Tales—Tape Talking

Hans Fantel, *Durable Pleasures, a Practical Guide to Better Tape Recording.* E. P. Dutton, New York, 1976. Chs. 2, 8, 13.

Art Spikol, *Magazine Writing: The Inside Angle.* Writer's Digest Books, Cincinnati, Ohio, 1979. Chs. 38, 39.

David Weitzman, *Underfoot.* Pp. 21–27.

4 The Plan's the Thing

Janice T. Dixon and Dora D. Flack, *Preserving Your Past.* Ch. 3.

Hayes B. Jacobs, *A Complete Guide to Writing and Selling Non-Fiction.* Writer's Digest, Cincinnati. Ch. XII.

Ken Macrorie, *Writing to Be Read.* Ch. 13.

5 Baiting the Hook—Beginnings
6 Wrapping It Up—Endings That Satisfy
(Beginnings and endings go together)

Connie Emerson, *Write on Target.* Writer's Digest Books, Cincinnati, 1981. Ch. 8.

Max Gunther, *Writing the Modern Magazine Article.* The Writer, Inc., 1973. Chs. 9, 14.

Ken Macrorie, *Writing to Be Read.* Pp. 96–100.

William Zinsser, *On Writing Well,* Second edition, Harper & Row, New York, 1980. Chs. 9, 10.

7 *A Title Is a Teaser*

Connie Emerson, *Write on Target*. Ch. 6.

Marjorie Holmes, *Writing the Creative Article*. The Writer, Inc., Boston, 1976. Ch. 7.

Kathryn M. Wilson, "Titles That Tantalize," *The Writer's Handbook* (edited by A. S. Burack). The Writer, Inc., Boston, 1976. Ch. 67.

8 *Show, Don't Tell*

Dorothea Brande, *Becoming a Writer*. Harcourt, Brace, New York, 1934. Ch. 11.

Janice T. Dixon and Dora D. Flack, *Preserving Your Past*. Doubleday, New York, 1977. Chs. 4, 5.

William J. Hoffman, *Life Writing: A Guide to Family Journals and Personal Memoirs*. Ch. VII, pp. 84–91.

Ken Macrorie, *Writing to Be Read*. Ch. 18.

9 *Flash Back, Move Forward*

Lois Duncan, *How to Write and Sell Your Personal Experiences*. Writer's Digest Books, Cincinnati, Ohio, 1979. Ch. 7, pp. 96–97.

Doris Ricker Marston, *A Guide to Writing History*. Writer's Digest Books, Cincinnati, 1976. Ch. 17, pp. 163–164.

10 *Vigorous Verbs*

Jefferson D. Bates, *Writing with Precision,* revised. Acropolis Books, Washington, D.C., 1978. Ch. 3.

Theodore M. Bernstein, *The Careful Writer*. Atheneum, New York, 1977. P. 13.

Henry Thomas, Ph.D., *Better English Made Easy*. Paperback edition, Fawcett Popular Library, New York, 1954. Ch. 4.

William Zinsser, *On Writing Well*. Ch. 13.

11 How to Keep Your Reader Awake

Louise Boggess, *Fiction Techniques That Sell*. Prentice-Hall, Englewood Cliffs, N.J., 1964. Pp. 184–187.

Rust Hills, *Writing in General and the Short Story in Particular*. Houghton Mifflin, Boston, 1977. Pp. 37–43.

A. S. Burack, editor, *The Writer's Handbook*. The Writer, Inc., Boston, 1970.

Ch. 48. Mary August Rodgers, "The Rhythm of a Story."

Ch. 51. Barbara Robinson, "What Happens? What If? What Then?"

Ch. 57. Vern Sneider, "The Impending Event."

12 To Repeat or Not to Repeat

Marjorie Holmes, *Writing the Creative Article*. Ch. 10, pp. 120–122.

Ken Macrorie, *Writing to Be Read*. Ch. 9.

13 Setting the Stage

A. S. Burack, editor, *The Writer's Handbook*.

Ch. 45. Elisabeth Ogilvie, "Background—the Most Important Character."

Ch. 54. Joan Williams, " 'You-Are-Thereness' in Fiction."

Rust Hills, *Writing in General and the Short Story in Particular.* Pp. 158–162.

Doris Ricker Marston, *A Guide to Writing History.* Pp. 139–141.

14 *A Real Live Character*

Louise Boggess, *Fiction Techniques That Sell.* Ch. 4.

Maren Elwood, *Characters Make Your Story.* The Writer, Inc., Boston, 1950. Chs. III–XVII.

Rust Hills, *Writing in General and the Short Story in Particular.* Pp. 43–49.

15 *Did They Really Say That?*

Maren Elwood, *Characters Make Your Story.* Ch. VII.

Ken Macrorie, *Writing to Be Read.* Ch. 6.

Doris Ricker Marston, *A Guide to Writing History.* Pp. 142–146.

16 *Spice Up Your Story—Use an Anecdote*

Louise Boggess, *How to Write Fillers and Short Features That Sell.* Harper & Row, New York, 1981. Chs. 2, 8, 10.

Marjorie Holmes, *Writing the Creative Article.* Pp. 28–30.

Max Gunther, *Writing the Modern Magazine Article.* Ch. 10.

17 Creeping Clutter

Jefferson D. Bates, *Writing with Precision.* Ch. 4.
Theodore M. Bernstein, *The Careful Writer.* Pp. 103, 179, 237, 480–483.
Ken Macrorie, *Writing to Be Read.* Ch. 14.

18 Engineering Your Memoir Road—Paragraphs

Theodore M. Bernstein, *The Careful Writer.* Pp. 324.
Max Gunther, *Writing the Modern Magazine Article.* Ch. 12.
Hayes B. Jacobs, *A Complete Guide to Writing and Selling Non-Fiction.* Pp. 178–183.
William Strunk, Jr., and E. B. White, *The Elements of Style,* third edition. Macmillan, New York, 1979. Pp. 15–19.

19 Sentences That Speed Your Journey

Jacques Barzun and Henry F. Graff, *The Modern Researcher,* revised edition. Harcourt, Brace & World, New York, 1970. Ch. 13.
Rudolph Flesch, *Say What You Mean.* Harper & Row, New York, 1972. Ch. 5.
Marilyn B. Gilbert, *Clear Writing.* Wiley, New York, 1972. Ch. 2.

20 Road Signs and Traffic Signals—Punctuation

Jefferson D. Bates, *Writing with Precision.* Revised. Pp. 160–161.
Theodore M. Bernstein, *The Careful Writer.* Pp. 356–373.

William Strunk, Jr., and E. B. White, *The Elements of Style*. Ch. I.

Jan Venolia, *Write Right!* Periwinkle Press, Woodland Hills, California, 1979. Ch. 3.

21 Write in Style—Your Own

Marjorie Holmes, *Writing the Creative Article*. Ch. 10.

Hayes B. Jacobs, *A Complete Guide to Writing and Selling Non-Fiction*. Ch. XV.

William Strunk, Jr., and E. B. White, *The Elements of Style*. Ch. V.

William Zinsser, *On Writing Well*. Ch. 4.

22 Analyze to Realize

Jacques Barzun and Henry F. Graff, *The Modern Researcher*. Pp. 310–311.

John Stahr, *The Byoir Style Book for Press Material*. Collier-Macmillan, New York, 1969. Pp. 24–25.

23 A Special Memoir—Sharing Your Travels

Connie Emerson, *Write on Target*. Pp. 195–199.

William Zinsser, *On Writing Well*. Ch. 12.

Louise Purwin Zobel, *The Travel Writer's Handbook*. Writer's Digest Books, Cincinnati, 1980. Ch. 13.

24 Try It Again and Again

Jacques Barzun, *Simple and Direct*. Harper & Row, New York, 1975. Ch. VI.

Lois Duncan, *How to Write and Sell Your Personal Experiences*. Ch. 6.

Ken Macrorie, *Writing to Be Read.* Ch. 12.

Art Spikol, *Magazine Writing: The Inside Angle.* Ch. 29.

25 Wrap Up a Neat Package

Janet T. Dixon and Dora D. Flack, *Preserving Your Past.* Chs. 20–22.

William J. Hoffman, *Life Writing: A Guide to Family Journals and Personal Memoirs.* Ch. XII.

26 An Unexpected Bonus

Janet T. Dixon and Dora D. Flack, *Preserving Your Past.* Chs. 18, 23.

William J. Hoffman, *Life Writing: A Guide to Family Journals and Personal Memoirs.* Ch. XIV.

MEMOIRS YOU MAY WANT TO READ

My students have learned from and enjoyed these books. I hope you too will enjoy them, as well as hundreds of others you will find at your library.

William C. Anderson, *The Two-Ton Albatross.* Crown, New York, 1969.

Anyone who has ever traveled in a trailer will appreciate this hilarious tale. A family travels across a transcontinental highway in a travel trailer with "two kids, two guppies, a miniature orange tree, a lobster, a St. Bernard dog and a claustrophobic wife." This story shows how to put humor into a memoir.

Richard Armour, *Golf Is a Four-Letter Word.* McGraw-Hill, New York, 1964.

Richard Armour, well-known for his prose satire and lighthearted verse, shares his humorous struggle to become a golfer. Later, he shares his even more hilarious struggle to give up his golf addiction. Both golfers and golf spectators will enjoy this delightful reminiscence.

Gwen Bagni and Paul Dubov, *Backstairs at the White House*. Bantam Books, New York, 1979.
Though listed as a novel, this story is based on the true experiences of a mother and daughter who served as maids in the White House. We glimpse the lives of eight presidents in some of their most intimate moments: Taft stuck in the bathtub, Coolidge checking the food in the kitchen, and Mrs. Eisenhower giving servants impossible tasks and then surprising them with a birthday party. Through the eyes of the two maids we see the presidents and their families as human beings.

Russell Baker, *Growing Up*. Congdon and Weed, New York, 1982.
This Pulitzer Prize–winning book is a real treasure. As the writer tells his sometimes sad, sometimes comic story, we really come to know those who influenced him. He gives us pictures of teachers and bullies, aunts and uncles, his little sister Doris, his grandmother, Ida Rebecca, and his mother fighting to survive the Depression. He shows his own coming of age during World War II and his on-again, off-again romance with his future wife. This warm and wonderful book has something for everyone.

Peg Bracken, *A Window Over the Sink*. Harcourt Brace Jovanovich, New York, 1981.
In this delightful book the author uses her new window

as an escape hatch to a kindlier time. In the warm Midwestern world she knew as a child, sex was a "many-colored mystery," pot something you cooked in, and *gay* a word that meant merry. With her lively writing, she takes you along as she dances through the past.

Ray Bradbury, *Dandelion Wine.* Doubleday, New York, 1957.

Ray Bradbury gives us a nostalgic look at the thrills, adventures and disappointments of a twelve-year-old boy one memorable summer. Though written as fiction, the boy's experiences are based on those of the author. The title comes from the dandelion wine he helped his grandfather make by gathering the dandelions. The writer's masterly use of similes and metaphors, specific details, and colorful descriptions help us to see and feel his delights and sorrows.

Gladys Hasty Carroll, *Only Fifty Years Ago.* Little, Brown, Boston, 1962.

This story, set in New England, paints a lively picture of a vibrant, loving family in the early days of the century. Beginning with January, the author takes us month by month through an exciting year. We meet Grandfather George; his hard-working son, Verd, and wife, Frankie; their children; and unmarried Aunt Vinnie. Maple syrup, mayflowers, July Fourth picnics, and an old-fashioned Christmas all come alive as the family celebrates. We find an interesting plan in this memoir, each chapter dealing with one month.

Colin Fletcher, *The Man Who Walked Through Time.* Knopf, New York, 1967.

From the moment Colin Fletcher saw the Grand Can-

yon he knew he must walk through it. An experienced
hiker, he wanted to do what no one had done before.
He shows us his problems, fears, people he meets, bur-
ros, and wild animals. As he becomes a part of the silence, the sand, the cliffs, the 200 million years that
have formed the great canyon, he finds a pattern of
man's place in nature. This is a grand story of an adventure.

Anne Frank: The Diary of a Young Girl. Doubleday, New
York, 1952.

Anne Frank's diary is a sensitive, moving story of a
young Jewish girl forced to hide with her family and
friends in Amsterdam during World War II. They find
safety in a crowded apartment above her father's ware-
house. Anne's diary shows us the fears, the day-to-day
problems, the occasional joys and fantasies of a teenager
struggling for her life. The book is a fine example of the
way a diary can become a revealing story of the past.

Frank B. Gilbreth, Jr., and Ernestine Gilbreth Carey,
Cheaper by the Dozen, updated. Crowell, New York,
1963.

This popular classic and bestseller, written by two
members of this delightful family, bring alive their wild
and hilarious antics during the first twenty-five years of
this century. In their easy, entertaining style, the writers show us school escapades, "shocking" bobbed hair
and high heels, and reckless trips in the family Pierce
Arrow. This updated edition adds a chapter on the
grownup Gilbreths and their children.

Helene Hanff, *84, Charing Cross Road.* Grossman, New
York, 1970.

Telling her amusing story entirely in letters, the writer shares her love affair with old, rare books. For twenty years she corresponds with the staff of Marks and Company, a London firm specializing in antique books. Their friendship grows as she buys more and more books and sends the company food parcels of luxuries hard to find in postwar England. This is a sparkling example of a memoir told through letters.

Helen Hayes, *On Reflection, An Autobiography.* M. Evans, New York, 1968.

In this autobiography, written entirely for her grandchildren, the queen of American theater opens her carefully guarded private world. We meet her grandmother "Grady" Hayes, with her exciting tales; her actress mother, who was "always chasing rainbows"; the actors and producers who guided her; and her romance with and marriage to the lovable but unpredictable Charles. The style is easy to read.

James Herriot, *All Things Bright and Beautiful.* St. Martin's Press, New York, 1974.

This is one of a series in which James Herriot, a veterinarian in rural England, reveals his love of animals and his work with them. We agonize with him over the death of a sheep. We are there as he struggles to save a prize bull. And we laugh at the bait he uses to lure a reluctant pig into its pen. We go along, too, when he courts his beloved Helen in his vintage car. His easy, natural style is a good model in writing our own memoirs. Notice his titles, too. Each one in the series is a line from a poem.

Marjorie Holmes, *You and I and Yesterday.* William Morrow, New York, 1973.

With this writer we journey back to a simpler time, when "everyone knew their neighbors." We feel the charm of yesterday in a small town in Iowa in the 1920s. We share games, peddlers, Monday-morning washday, all-day suckers, Chautauqua, and the first family car. Her stories will help trigger your own memories of a time "when the American dream still beckoned."

Helen Hoover, *The Years of the Forest.* Knopf, New York, 1973.

Helen Hoover shows the challenges as well as the delights she and her husband meet in creating their wilderness home. Their deep love for the forest and for the animals they befriend helps them to cope with the many problems in the sixteen years it took to reach their goal. This sensitive, moving story of adventure, joy, and sorrow is for all who love the out-of-doors.

Peter Jenkins, *A Walk Across America.* William Morrow, 1979.

Disillusioned like most of his generation, young Peter Jenkins sets out with his dog, Cooper, to discover the real America. He meets down-to-earth people, such as a mountain hermit, a delightful black family, and the girl he eventually marries. He finds, too, a new pride in his country and faith in God and man. In this inspiring story the first chapter is a good example of a flashback beginning.

Rose Fitzgerald Kennedy, *Times to Remember.* Doubleday, New York, 1974.

Written by the matriarch of the family, this is the only book about Kennedys written by a Kennedy. The writer recalls memories of the loves, the joys, the tragedies of the Kennedy clan. We see through her eyes the events that influenced history. In her letters and those of her family, in excerpts from school essays, in poems from children and grandchildren we share a very human side of this famous family.

Catherine Marshall, *To Live Again.* McGraw-Hill, New York, 1957.

Beginning with the death of her famous husband, Catherine Marshall writes of her struggle to meet the sudden challenges thrust upon her. In this book she gives us intimate stories of loving friends, laughter and despair, family and home. Through her unswerving faith she finds strength and inspiration to meet life's most difficult challenges.

Catherine Hanf Noren, *The Camera of My Family.* Knopf, New York, 1976.

This is a book that is different, the 100-year album of a German-Jewish family who treasured mementos. Documents, news clips, letters, photos, and stories of five generations bring history alive. From peaceful alpine vacations to the escape from Hitler's Germany, it is a graphic account of one family. Study it for fine examples of ways to use mementos in your own memoirs.

Norman Rockwell, *Norman Rockwell,* My Adventures as an Illustrator. As told to Thomas Rockwell. Doubleday, New York, 1960.

We meet the famous artist as a mischievous boy, in and out of trouble, painfully conscious of the difference money can make. Struggling through art school, he held strange jobs such as drawing the stages of a baby's development in a room lined with bottled fetuses. He learned to bring ordinary people alive in his paintings, and his book brings him alive as a lovable person. It is a good example of an as-told-to memoir.

Richard Rodriguez, *Hunger of Memory.* David R. Godine, Boston, 1982.
Richard Rodriguez, growing up in a Spanish-speaking family in Sacramento, California, tells a sensitive story. He shares his struggles as he learns the difference between his family's "private" language and "public English." Awarded college scholarships, he earns degrees both from American and English universities yet chooses to write rather than teach. His honest, eloquent writing gives a new understanding of bilingual and affirmative-action programs. This is a brave and beautifully written memoir.

John Steinbeck, *Travels with Charley.* Viking, New York, 1962.
This master of the written word takes us along in his camper on his journey to find what America between the oceans is like. With his "old French gentleman poodle, Charley," he camps by lakes, in forests, in deserts. He meets and talks with migrant workers, farmers, tradespeople, city policemen, park rangers—anyone who will stop. We learn to know them all as he journeys from New York to San Francisco and back. Steinbeck's writing carries us along from page to page, a fine example of a memoir.

Jesse Stuart, *The Thread That Runs So True.* Charles Scribner's Sons, New York, 1958.
Jesse Stuart began teaching in a dilapidated one-room schoolhouse when he was only seventeen. A teacher in

Lonesome Valley, Kentucky, had to be a real man. He not only had to teach fifty-four classes each day. He also had to fight the older and bigger pupils, paint the schoolhouse himself, and milk the cows where he boarded. His story is an inspiration both to students and teachers.

Jade Snow Wong, *Fifth Chinese Daughter.* Harper & Brothers, New York, 1950.

Writing in the third person, according to Chinese custom, Jade Snow Wong tells the story of growing up in a Chinese family in an American world. Her father's fifth daughter, she shows with humor and insight her struggle to adjust her family's Old World customs to New World ideas. She paints lively pictures of the people around her in Chinatown and the disapproval and wonder as she sets out to have her own career. Searching for her destiny, she finally becomes one of America's leading artist-ceramists. In spite of conflict, she tells her story joyfully.

Index

Acknowledgments

Grateful acknowledgment is made for permission to reprint:

Excerpt from "Try A Love Account" by Fanny-Maude Evans. Reprinted from the September 1975 issue of *Lady's Circle.*

Excerpt from "Whatever Happened to the Good Old Middy Blouse?" by Robin Worthington. Reprinted from the September 15, 1974 issue of Seattle *Post-Intelligencer Northwest.*

Excerpt from "Just This Side of Byzantium, An Introduction" from *Dandelion Wine* by Ray Bradbury. Copyright © 1975 by Ray Bradbury. Reprinted by permission of Don Congdon Associates, Inc.

Excerpt from "Wild N. Y. Hostage Parade" by Pete Hamill reprinted from the January 31, 1981 issue of the San Francisco *Chronicle.*

Excerpt from "A Rare and Special Place" by T. H. Watkins. Reprinted from the April 6, 1975 issue of *California Living Magazine.* Copyright © 1975 by California Living Magazine. Reprinted by permission of California Living Magazine and the author.

Excerpt from an interview with Isaac Bashevis Singer by Helen Benedict. Reprinted from the May 1980 issue of *Writer's Digest.* Reprinted by permission of Isaac Bashevis Singer.

Excerpt from "Age: 101—Motto: Go Do!" by Peggy Mann, *Reader's Digest,* August 1978. Reprinted by permission of Reader's Digest.

Excerpt from "Pas de Deux" by Robert Orben, *Reader's Digest,* June 1981. Originally appeared in *Orben's Current Comedy,* May 23, 1974. Reprinted by permission of Reader's Digest and the author.

Excerpt from "The Happy Hacker" by Jim Bishop, *Reader's Digest,* August 1978. Reprinted by permission of Reader's Digest.

Excerpts from "Chicken Soup" by Jayne Vosti; "Desert Postmistress" by Sue Scofield; "First Day of School in 1917" by Leona Cox; "The Indelicate Delicacy" by Doris Bona; "Innocents Abroad in New York" by Rozilla Reed; "A Lesson in Silver" by Charles W. Reed; "My First Wedding Day" by Elfriede Tavernier; "My Most Prized Possession" by Eugene J. Tavernier; "The Night Hunters" by Marjorie Heilbron; "Old Nic" by Doris Bona; "Primordial Adventure" by Louise Mohr; "Revolt Against Starting School" by Ferol M. Slotte; "A Talent For Cutting" by Avis Kurtzweil; "The Winker" by Helen Drechsler from *Silhouettes of the Past.* Copyright 1980 Mountain View-Los Altos Adult School. Reprinted by permission.

Excerpt from "The Conscientious Elves of Hawaii" originally appeared in *Passages.*

Excerpts from "Love Cards" and "A Very Special Dinner" originally appeared in *Guideposts.*

"The Magic Map" originally appeared in *Odyssey.*

Excerpt from "The Christmas Letter" originally appeared in *The Lookout.*

Excerpts from "A Blanket of Love" and "Second Half, Second Chance" originally appeared in the *Lutheran Women*.

Excerpt from "A Valentine for Dixie" originally appeared in *Catholic Digest*.

Excerpts from "A Different Kind of Rainbow" originally appeared in *Elks Magazine*.

The following selections are published here for the first time:

Excerpt from "The Storm" by Esther C. Clifton.
Excerpt from "Anecdote" by Helen R. Creighton.
Excerpt from "Sky Farmers" by Zella L. Edwards.
Excerpt from "A Storm" by Dahl C. Phelps.
Excerpt from "A Storm" by Katherine D. Shelley.
Excerpt from "A Storm" by Richard Vanderlippe.
Excerpt from "A Poem" by Evan Wild.